SACRED SELF-CARE

Sacred Self-Care

Daily Practices for
Nurturing Our Whole Selves

CHANEQUA WALKER-BARNES, PhD

HARPERONE

An Imprint of HarperCollins*Publishers*

HarperCollins books may be purchased for educational, business, or sales promotional use. For information, please email the Special Markets Department at SPsales@harpercollins.com.

FIRST EDITION

Designed by Bonni Leon-Berman

Library of Congress Cataloging-in-Publication Data has been applied for.

ISBN 978-0-06-328713-6

23 24 25 26 27 LBC 5 4 3 2 1

For Delwin,

whose love has helped me to love myself, and

for Yusef, who left us too soon

CONTENTS

INTRODUCTION

Self-Care as a Way of Life

The idea for this book began in early 2021, as we were nearing the end of the first full year of the COVID-19 pandemic. As we approached Ash Wednesday that year, a time when Christians were reflecting on the upcoming season of Lent and what they might give up as a spiritual practice, I recognized how we had already given up so much: hugs, meals, and holiday gatherings with friends and family; learning, working, and worshipping in person; team sports and other group extracurricular activities; movies, vacations, and trips to theme parks; Easter egg hunts, trick-or-treating, and Christmas dinners; proms, graduations, birthday parties, and weddings; visiting loved ones in hospitals and nursing homes; and even comforting one another at funerals. It was a season when *taking on* nourishing practices felt so much more urgent than the act of *giving up*. This season taught me that taking on practices that nourish and enrich our spiritual and physical selves, or self-care in the deepest sense, actually *strengthens* our capacity to serve God, practices that can help us in all of our seasons.

The fact that this all started in a Lenten season is significant. I did not grow up observing Lent as a liturgical season (you can read more of this story in the back of this book, in "Using This Book for Lent"). Before I went to seminary in 2004, I had never heard of the liturgical calendar. During my second year in seminary, I threw myself headlong into the Lenten observance. I ate pancakes for dinner on Shrove Tuesday, awkwardly walked around with palm ashes on my forehead on Ash Wednesday, walked out of a United Methodist church in utter silence at the end of a Good Friday service, and worshipped at dawn in the frigid outside air on Easter Sunday. I loved every bit of it. To this day, I love Lent as much as I love Advent.

Every year since then, I have approached Lent prayerfully and thoughtfully. As I consider fasting, I ask myself the same question that I asked my seminary classmates when I first learned about Lent: "What's the point?" I took seriously the invitation that Lent offered to draw closer to God and to strengthen my capacity to serve God in the world.

That, in essence, is what I think Lent is about: it is an invitation to develop and strengthen practices that enhance the depth of our discipleship and our ministry in the world. Sometimes that means abnegation—giving up material pleasures, activities that we enjoy, or habits that have become addictive or counterproductive. Habits can be tangible things (like chocolate or social media or video games), but they can also be intangible practices, tendencies, or ways of being in the world. We might, for example, need to give up toxic positivity, the forced optimism that hides our true feelings and prevents us from being authentic with God and with other people. We may need to relinquish perfectionism, not the kind that Christ teaches us to strive for when he called us to be perfect in our love for one another (Matt. 5:48), in our charity and trust in God's provision rather than in the riches of this world (Matt. 19:21), and in our unity (John 17:2). The kind of perfection we need to give up is the kind that tempts us to believe that we are (or ought to be) inhuman, infallible, and inerrant.

The thing is, abnegation does not necessarily strengthen discipleship. Giving up something does not teach us what we need to do or be, only what we need *not* to do or be. Very often, when we give up something that is counterproductive, it leaves a void that we then fill, often unwittingly, with yet another counterproductive habit. This is why people who quit using recreational drugs might end up smoking cigarettes, or why people who quit smoking cigarettes might end up overeating. Thoughtful Lenten disciplines, then, need to be about more than *giving up* unproductive practices; they should also involve *taking on* practices that nourish and enrich us, practices that usher us not toward death but toward resurrection. Because, ultimately, that is what Lent is about: death yielding to resurrection. In fact, it is what Christian discipleship is about. We give up counterproductive, unjust, and unholy ways of being so that we can take on the deeper, richer, fuller life that Christ offers us.

The beauty of this approach is that this spiritual formation does not have to be limited to the forty-seven days between

Ash Wednesday and Easter Sunday. I have never understood why Lenten disciplines end at Easter. After all, if they are supposed to be good for our relationship with God, why wouldn't we keep doing them? Maybe it is because we have made Lenten disciplines all about death and self-denial. While Lent is a special opportunity for remembering Christ's suffering, its practices should always remind us that we are a resurrection people. This is what Christian spiritual disciplines do: they point us *to* and *through* resurrection in everyday life.

When I began observing Lent, I quickly realized that my discipleship required a different type of fast, an ongoing one. I wanted a year-round practice that would help me to live into Christ's resurrection promises in the midst of a world that continuously offers death.

I am a two-time breast cancer survivor from an extended family that has lost several people to the disease. I am technically cancer free but also keenly aware that a stray cancer cell could lurk somewhere in my body, waiting to attack again. Awareness of the possibility of early death is with me daily. I need a practice that ushers me into resurrection.

I am an African American woman, a survivor of the transatlantic slave trade, living in the South during the resurgence of White Christian nationalism, when the names of Black people killed by the police become hashtags on a regular basis, and when a right-wing-controlled Supreme Court is eroding civil rights and environmental justice. Awareness of the possibility of unjust death is with me daily. I need a practice that ushers me into resurrection.

I am an American living in the time of the COVID-19 pandemic, when news of the deaths of extended family and friends arrives regularly, when every encounter with an unmasked and unvaccinated person poses a threat to me and my family. Awareness of the possibility of needless death is with me daily. I need a practice that ushers me into resurrection. I offer this devotional, then, for other people who need to be ushered into resurrection in the midst of a death-dealing world.

Self-Care as a Spiritual Discipline

My journey to self-care has been long, with twists and turns along the way. It began in 2002. I was on the fast track to tenure and success in my second year as a clinical psychology professor, where I had achieved the rare feat of applying for and receiving a prestigious federally funded grant in my first year. My colleagues marveled at how well I handled the stresses of the job, but beneath the well-dressed, unflappable exterior, I was crumbling. My medical chart was starting to fill up—hypertension, recurrent and inexplicable pain, insomnia, weight gain, fibroids, and infertility. What wasn't in the chart were the emotional issues—loneliness, anxiety, irritability.

It all came to a head at Thanksgiving. Months earlier, my partner and I had decided to forgo the usual celebration and to spend the holiday in a bed-and-breakfast for some much-needed rest and relaxation. But when my family asked to hold dinner at our new North Carolina home, I couldn't say no. I didn't even know it was an option. In addition to being the firstborn child of a single mother, I am the oldest grandchild on both sides of my family. Since I was ten, I've been taking care of siblings, cousins, even the children of family friends. "Take care of your mother," one of my uncles used to tell me every time we said goodbye. "But what about me?" I would wonder silently.

In the midst of my pain, stress, and fatigue, my partner and I spent weeks preparing to host the twenty-something aunts, uncles, and cousins who had said they were coming. On Thanksgiving Day, two people showed up—my father and my youngest brother. I was devastated. *Why hadn't they shown up for me? Why did it seem that no one (except my partner) showed up for me? I was tired of caring for everyone else. Who was going to care for me?* Then it hit me: I had to take care of me. And I had to model to others how they should care for me.

So I embarked on a journey to self-care with a few small changes: affirmations, daily prayer and meditation, regular exercise, and breaks during my day. Within weeks, I felt better physically and emotionally. I felt more secure in my own identity and more connected to other people. But there was an unanticipated benefit: I felt more connected to God. It turned out that the more I cared for myself, the more I wanted to serve God in the world.

Self-care may seem to be an odd focus for a Christian devotional. After all, we typically think of spiritual disciplines as . . . well, spiritual. That is, they are focused upon the transcendent—God, the Spirit, Jesus Christ, the afterlife. Self-care, in contrast, is very much grounded in the earthly, in the flesh, in the body, in the here and now. Many of us have learned to think of the human spirit and body in dualistic ways. It is common to hear Christians talk about the *spiritual man*, as distinct from the *natural man*. But there is no such distinction. We are not spirits that are simply housed in bodies. We are our bodies. There can be no spiritual life that does not engage the body.

In her book *Soul Feast*, Marjorie Thompson defines the spiritual life in this way: "Scripturally speaking, the spiritual life is simply the increasing vitality and sway of God's Spirit in us. It is a magnificent choreography of the Holy Spirit in the human spirit, moving us toward communion with both Creator and creation. The spiritual life is thus grounded in relationship. It has to do with God's way of relating to us and our way of responding to God."[1] Notice the words that Thompson uses: *sway, choreography, moving, grounded, responding*. These are kinetic words. They are words about movement, about embodiment. Spirituality is embodied.

This book, then, is about sacred self-care—the practices we engage in to develop and nurture ourselves as beings who are beautifully and wonderfully created by God in God's own image and likeness. As a clinical psychologist, pastor, and activist, I have studied and worked with people over the years to encourage them to think of self-care as both a divine right and a sacred obligation. I have used self-care as a clinical intervention with therapy clients. I have encouraged clergy, seminary faculty, faith-based activists, and other Christian leaders to view self-care as a strategy for sustaining the work that God has called them to do. I even teach a graduate course on self-care at my seminary, in the hope that helping seminarians develop healthy practices now will reduce their risk of ministry burnout in the years to come. Over the next seven weeks, we will look at what our divine creation means for our relationship with our bodies, particularly how we care for ourselves. We will identify some of the barriers and obstacles that prevent us from exercising care of our sacred selves. We will explore practices that will help us to shift our attitudes and behaviors toward our care.

Self-care is an anachronistic concept for biblical times. The biblical characters and writers, in contrast to our postindustrial society, lived in a time when most of the day's work focused on growing, producing, and securing everything they needed to live. People did not need guidelines on how to eat well because everything was sustainable and seasonal. Exercise was an irrelevant concept because most people would have walked and worked throughout their entire day. So the biblical authors would have had no framework for thinking about self-care the way that we do. Nevertheless, as with other topics, there is plenty of biblical wisdom to be found that connects to our self-care journeys. Finding it sometimes requires employing a generous interpretative framework, one in which we read texts with the assumption that God wants humanity (and all of creation) to flourish and thrive, not to suffer needlessly. In other words, I invite you to be open to the wisdom we can glean from scripture when it comes to caring for ourselves.

This book is an invitation into a journey toward sacred self-care. Just as wellness is wholistic, self-care is, too. Sacred self-care, then, integrates our spiritual, physical, emotional, mental, and relational well-being. In lieu of rote prescriptions about what you need to do in order to care for yourself, this book offers practices and reflections to help you discern your body's Spirit-given wisdom about what you need to be well, not only for your own sake but also to sustain you for the work that God has called you to do in the world, whether that is being a pastor, a parent, an activist, a student, or a retired grandparent. It invites you to deepen self-care practices that you may already have in place and to try on new practices to see if they are helpful to you. You don't have to make a commitment to anything. Just try it on and see if it fits; keep what does and discard what does not. It is my prayerful hope that at the end of our seven-week journey, you will have developed both a plan and a proclivity to continue practicing sacred self-care throughout your life.

How to Use This Book

While inspired by Lent, this book is designed to be used at any time in the year. It includes seven weeks of daily devotionals, each of which is devoted to a different theme.

The devotionals follow a similar pattern each week. Each day's devotional and each week's theme builds upon what precedes it, so it's best to follow the devotionals sequentially. But if you miss a day, you can combine two of them (especially on a weekday). It's okay to be imperfect. Self-care is imperfect and flexible. Humans are imperfect and ideally also flexible.

The book is designed for each week to start on Monday, but if, for example, you work on weekends and it's better for you to align day 6 or 7 with your days off, do what works best. You could also choose to spread it out longer than seven weeks. If you experience a disruption, just pick back up whenever you are ready.

The first six days of each week have a scripture reading, a brief reflection on the theme, and a short practice that is designed to be accomplished within that day. No money or special equipment or materials are needed, just a bit of time and energy. The practices on day 6 (Saturdays if you use a Monday start) will often require more time but are still doable within a day. The seventh day of each week (Sundays for most people) follows a different format: a scripture reading, a reflection on the theme, a prayer and silent meditation, a hymn, and a benediction. The hymns can be read or sung silently or aloud. The lyrics are included, and I also provide the hymn numbers from the *African American Heritage Hymnal.*[2] After all, if you're going to sing them, you should do it right (I promise this will be the only time that I judge you in this book).

If you are using this as a Lenten devotional, feel free to observe the practices on their own or in combination with other practices, including traditional fasts. Start on the Monday before Ash Wednesday (so Ash Wednesday would be day 3), and the final day will line up with Easter Sunday. Consider adding the readings from the Revised Common Lectionary to your Sunday observance.[3] A listing of the lectionary readings, along with a brief explanation, is in the back of this book.

You will benefit most by reading the devotional in the morning. Some of the practices require you to do something; others require trying on new ideas or perhaps observing and reflecting upon your patterns for the day as you go about your normal activity. Thus, it's best to know what the practice is before you start your day. At the same time, because self-care is personal, all of the practices have flexibility built into them. They will be challenging but realistic and time-limited enough to incorporate in a workday or a busy day with family. Establishing a regular routine of reading the devotional in the morning will help you to develop the discipline of setting aside protected time for self-care that won't be impinged upon by your normal relationships and responsibilities. This may mean getting up earlier than normal, especially if you share living space with partners, children, extended family, or roommates. Sometimes it's the mere presence of other people who want and need to talk with us in the mornings that competes with self-care routines (although, as we'll see, spending time with people we love is also self-care)!

The daily practices frequently involve the use of affirmations to reshape how we think about ourselves and our self-care. Affirmations are a form of cognitive reframing that help us to recognize and replace maladaptive thought patterns with positive and self-nurturing beliefs that empower us to behave differently. For example, one of my recurrent maladaptive thoughts is "I don't have enough time for self-care this morning because I need to hurry up and get to work." That thought is not only unhelpful (because it prevents me from engaging in practices that are beneficial to my health) but also untrue (because even just a few minutes of meditation or stretching is beneficial, and I have considerable flexibility in my schedule most days). So I work to replace that thought with one that is true and helpful, such as "Time is God's plentiful gift to me." You can practice each affirmation simply by saying it multiple times. You might also write your affirmations on a small card to carry with you to remind yourself throughout the day. Better yet: set a reminder using your smartphone.

There are specific opportunities for journaling and written reflection throughout the study as well, and if you'd like, you could consider keeping a journal alongside the book.

The point is to challenge yourself but to make it work for you and the demands of your life, including any physical or emotional constraints that you have. Change the practices whenever you feel the need. Just try to do something for your own benefit each day. Remember, the only day that the body has is today. But also remember: every day is a new opportunity to practice self-care. Morning by morning, new mercies we see.

WEEK 1

Understanding Sacred Self-Care

Self-care is all the rage these days. It is hard to watch television without some commercial promising you that for the right price point, you, too, can enjoy a life of care-free frolicking in the grass with your golden retriever and your grandchildren. From Botox injections to jade yoni eggs to every flavor of sheet mask imaginable, corporations are inventing all kinds of ways to cash in on the self-care hype. It's enough to induce self-care fatigue in anyone. But the idea that self-care is dependent upon a product—or even upon money—is a misperception, and a dangerous one at that. Developing sustainable self-care practices requires knowing what self-care is and how it connects to Christian discipleship.

This week, we'll kick off our self-care journey by understanding what self-care is and what it is not and reflecting on what self-care needs to look like specifically for you.

DAY 1

Self-Care
Is Gratitude

You are the one who created my innermost parts;
you knit me together while I was still in my mother's womb.
I give thanks to you that I was marvelously set apart.
Your works are wonderful—I know that very well.

PSALM 139:13–14

Have you ever bought, crafted, or cooked something for another
person only to have them reject it, discard it, or treat it carelessly? If you're a caregiver or parent to tweens or teenagers,
you probably know this feeling well. Seriously, what kind of
person buys new clothing and then comes home and dumps it
on the floor? Or wears brand-name *white* sneakers to a Scouts

meeting where they know they will be tramping in mud? Or wears a hard-to-find hoodie so often that it wears out within a few weeks of purchase? See, this is why you can't have nice things! . . . My bad, my parenting stress got triggered.

I wonder if this is what it is like for God watching us neglect ourselves, the selves that God created and pronounced good. "God saw everything he had made: it was supremely good" (Gen. 1:31). According to Psalm 139, our lives are not the result of some heavenly factory where humans are mass-produced on an assembly line. God takes the time to individually craft each of us, to knit us together while we are yet in the womb, down to our innermost parts. Each one of us is uniquely and wonderfully handmade. We even have the imperfections that often come from handmade crafting!

While the psalmist's description is not meant to be a literal explanation of the reproduction process, it is a beautiful image that conveys an important truth that scripture wants us to understand: each and every one of us is God's perfect gift.

Our *self*—the body-mind-spirit that makes up who we are and that shapes our experiences of the world—is God's first and best gift to each one of us. How we care for ourselves is our response of gratitude for that gift. Each day we wake up, we are given that gift anew, and we have another opportunity to show our appreciation for it.

Unfortunately, many of us have, without even realizing it or meaning to, responded to God's gift in the same way that an entitled teenager might. It is not that we're bad or even ungrateful. We simply don't recognize the value of the gift. So we don't place the right priority on it. We treat it carelessly, trampling

it on the ground, exposing it to destructive elements, using it
for the wrong purposes, or wearing it out as we push it beyond
its capacity. We neglect ourselves, abuse ourselves, and exhaust
ourselves, believing that other people and institutions are more
important than we are. Sometimes we even do this in the name
of God as we serve our churches and communities.

But we are God's good and perfect gift. We *are* the good thing.
Just imagine what our self-care might look like if we believed
that.

Today's Practice

Repeat the following affirmation to yourself ten times: *I am
created in the image of God. I am God's perfect gift.* For an added
challenge, sit or stand in front of a mirror for two or three
minutes and repeat it aloud as you look at yourself, taking a
deep breath between each repetition. A full-length mirror
is ideal, but even a handheld mirror will work. If this brings
up negative or shameful thoughts about your body, notice
your feelings and breathe deeply through them. If you start
to feel overwhelmed, honor your feelings and pause. Instead,
you could focus your eyes on a part of the body that you feel
comfortable with (even if it's just your fingernail), or you can
close your eyes and skip the mirror altogether.

DAY 2

Self-Care Is Self-Love

You were called to freedom, brothers and sisters; only
don't let this freedom be an opportunity to indulge
your selfish impulses, but serve each other through love.
All the Law has been fulfilled in a single statement:
Love your neighbor as yourself.

GALATIANS 5:13–14

Two weeks after my thirtieth birthday, I hit a physical and
mental breaking point, a vortex of acute back and neck pain,
high blood pressure, weight gain, insomnia, and chronic self-
doubt that was exacerbated by, if not caused by, self-neglect.
I had a habit of putting other people's needs ahead of my own,
promising myself that I would focus on myself after everything

else was done. But it was never done. The more I did, the more people wanted me to do. After all, why wouldn't they? I was highly dependable, self-reliant, and skilled—just the type of person you could give something to and trust that it would be done.

It didn't help that I had internalized the idea that it was my Christian duty to serve others above all else, that service and suffering were opportunities for salvation and sanctification. I thought it was a sign of God's favor that my service was so highly desired by my employer, my family, my church, and my community. And I definitely didn't want to block God's blessing!

Unfortunately, I'd come to learn I was not alone in these beliefs. The first time I taught about self-care for my congregation's women's ministry in early 2003, several women confessed that they had trouble caring for themselves because it felt selfish. In the twenty years since, I've heard that sentiment more than I can count. Until recently, in fact, if you started typing "self-care is" into the Google search bar, the first autocompletion option would be "selfish."

Self-care is not selfish. It is not about being exclusively focused upon our needs, pleasure, and well-being without consideration of or regard for others, which is how dictionaries define selfishness. When we recognize our self as a sacred gift of God who is meant to be in relationship with other beings who are also wonderfully and beautifully made in the image of God, self-care becomes a fulfillment of the second part of the Great Commandment: "Love your neighbor as yourself." Self-care is self-love.

When Jesus responded to the legal expert's question about what is necessary to gain eternal life in Luke 10, he assumed self-love as evident. Love of self, therefore, is not at odds with love of others. Jesus underscores this idea twice more in Luke 10: first in the telling of the parable of the Good Samaritan, whose care for a wounded stranger did not prevent him from continuing his own journey; and second in his praise of Mary for practicing presence, in contrast to Martha's frantic servanthood. Paul reiterates the theme in Galatians, telling us that while selfishness is a hindrance to both freedom and love of neighbor, self-love is a prerequisite for neighbor love.

Today's Practice

Think about someone whom you deeply love and for whom you wish the very best in life. It could be a child, a partner, a sibling, a friend, or even a younger version of yourself. What would you tell this person about caring for themself? How do your wishes for that person differ from how you currently care for yourself? Once you've identified the answers to these questions, is there one way you could choose to show yourself self-love today?

DAY 3

Self-Care Is Stewardship

Those who have much will receive more, and they will have more than they need. But as for those who don't have much, even the little bit they have will be taken away from them.

MATTHEW 25:29

One of my least favorite parables has been the parable of the talents (Matt. 25:14–30). It's a weird story that Jesus told his disciples about a wealthy man who, right before going on a journey, entrusted three of his servants with differing amounts of money to steward during his absence. When he returned, he asked each of them to account for what they had done. The two given the most money had invested it and made more.

But the one with the least had stored it away for safekeeping, prompting his master's wrath.

I've heard this story preached and taught a lot, and to me it seemed to contradict Christ's eschewing of material wealth and his generosity to the poor. It was only when I began thinking about this parable in relation to self-care that it began to make sense to me. Because self-care is fundamentally about steward-ship.

Stewardship is a word we use in a lot of different contexts—churches, business and financial settings, even relationships—without often defining what it means. Merriam-Webster's dictionary defines stewardship as "the careful and responsible management of something entrusted to one's care." If we think about that definition in relation to self-care, then sacred self-care is the act of stewarding ourselves, including our bodies, minds, and spirits—the wondrous gifts that have been entrusted to us by God. It turns out that some strings are attached when the Divine gives gifts, as the parable of the talents so clearly shows us.

I think that God is brokenhearted, not angry (as we see in the parable), when we neglect and mistreat ourselves. But there is a natural order of cause and effect that happens with self-care. Just as God put care into creating us, our divinely knit selves require the same type of thoughtful care from us during our lives. It's not just that we deserve self-care; we need it. When we fail to steward ourselves well, our body has a way of responding with its own wrath: we experience illness, mental health problems, broken relationships, and so on. Our capacity for ministry diminishes, maybe even leading to spiritual, physical, and emotional burnout.

The more we steward ourselves with good care, the more we thrive, not just physically but also spiritually, mentally, and emotionally. We don't reach perfection. We will still go through struggles, but we will face them with more physical, spiritual, mental, and emotional resources. If life is a marathon, we may not run the entire race, but we can at least run the leg of the race that has been entrusted to us. Indeed, we can run it with greater faithfulness, vitality, and, possibly, effectiveness.

Today's Practice

Repeat the following affirmation to yourself ten times: *I am a good steward of my body, mind, and spirit.* Continue to repeat it to yourself at intervals throughout the day.

DAY 4

Self-Care Is Wellness

Meanwhile, a man crippled since birth was being carried in. Every day, people would place him at the temple gate known as the Beautiful Gate so he could ask for money from those entering the temple. When he saw Peter and John about to enter, he began to ask them for a gift. Peter and John stared at him. Peter said, "Look at us!" So the man gazed at them, expecting to receive something from them. Peter said, "I don't have any money, but I will give you what I do have. In the name of Jesus Christ the Nazarene, rise up and walk!"

ACTS 3:2–6

Like the crippled man who lay at the Beautiful Gate, we have been taught by our consumption-focused culture to look for self-care in the wrong places: pedicures, spa days, a round of golf, a day of shopping, a weekend getaway, a luxury skin-care product. Capitalism has taken over the idea of self-care, making us think that it is something we buy, consume, or travel to. To be clear, treating ourselves is important and can be part of our self-care tool kit. But it is not the central focus.

Sacred self-care is about wellness, that is, maximizing our spiritual, physical, emotional, mental, relational, financial, and vocational health and well-being. We do this both for our own sake and so that we might sustain our vitality as agents of God's mission of justice, mercy, and peace in the world. Self-care enables us to participate in this mission in ways that are faithful, effective, imaginative, and sustainable. Just as the practice of self-care varies from person to person, so does our personal definition of the wellness we strive for. For some of us, the pursuit of physical wellness might mean being able to go for a walk. For others, it might mean being able to run a marathon. And for some of us, it may simply mean having fewer pain-filled days.

Self-care, then, consists of the activities, habits, disciplines, and thought patterns that we integrate into our life on a regular basis to maximize our capacity for wellness given our circumstances, ability and disability, and personal history. Some practices are daily; others are weekly, monthly, quarterly, or yearly. But self-care is part of everyday life. It includes how we rest, move, and feed our bodies; how we cultivate loving, mutually beneficial relationships; how we nurture our sense of connection to the Spirit; how we experience joy and honor our emotions; and how we manage our commitments so that our output is not greater than our input.

Think about car maintenance. It's nice to get your car de-tailed, to add a personalized license plate, and to upgrade the sound system. But those are luxuries that have nothing to do with the car's functioning. You can do all that and end up with a beautiful but broken-down vehicle! Self-care is more like keeping gas in the car, checking the oil and fluids, and protecting it from environmental hazards like snow, salt, and bad drivers. Less sexy, sure, but crucial to keeping the car running so we can get to where we need to go.

Today's Practice

Pay attention to the self-care practices that you are already doing in each of these areas: physical, emotional, spiritual, mental, and relational well-being. Today is a good time to evaluate how you are doing in each of these areas, using the Sacred Self-Care Inventory in the back of this book. You don't need to change anything today. Just notice where you are, what you are already doing, and where you think you could improve.

DAY 5

Self-Care Is Subversive

Hear this, you who trample on the needy and destroy the poor of the land, saying, "When will the new moon be over so that we may sell grain, and the Sabbath so that we may offer wheat for sale, make the ephah smaller, enlarge the shekel, and deceive with false balances, in order to buy the needy for silver and the helpless for sandals, and sell garbage as grain?"

AMOS 8:4-6

Self-care should be the most natural thing in the world. We should be innately inclined to devote a significant part of our time and energy to caring for ourselves—taking the time to prepare, cook, and eat nutritious meals; moving our bodies in ways that challenge and restore us; getting good sleep; spending time with people whom we love and who love us; spending time in prayer and meditation; and experiencing joy and pleasure. Instead, we find ourselves fighting to carve out space and time to sustain our own lives!

This is not an accident. It's the product of living in a hyper-capitalist society built on a slave economy, which reduced people to commodities to be exploited. The logic of this economy persists today. It teaches all of us that our worth is dependent upon our productivity and our service to others. It teaches us to prioritize our jobs, roles, and responsibilities over ourselves. This might make sense if most of our responsibilities were related to people who love and support us in return. But capitalism devalues that, too, instead teaching us to dedicate ourselves to corporate entities—companies, organizations, universities, and, yes, even churches. It teaches us to disregard or rush through Sabbath rest so that we can quickly return to offering wheat for sale, making the ephah smaller, and enlarging the shekel.

A hyper-capitalist economy is disinterested in the survival and well-being of anyone beyond their utility as workers. Making the commitment to self-care forces a radical shift in our priorities that subverts the logic of capitalism. This is what Audre Lorde realized after cancer had spread through her body. It was then she realized that health and survival were acts of defiance for people who were never meant to survive, especially the survivor-descendants of the transatlantic slave trade and Native American genocide. Lorde wrote:

I had to examine, in my dreams as well as in my immune-
function tests, the devastating effects of overextension.
Overextending myself is not stretching myself. I had
to accept how difficult it is to monitor the difference.
Necessary for me as cutting down on sugar. Crucial.
Physically. Psychically. Caring for myself is not self-
indulgence, it is self-preservation, and that is an act of
political warfare.[1]

Sacred self-care is not an act of indulgence; it is an act of
resistance. Much like Sabbath keeping, self-care subverts the
beliefs that we must do and be *more*; that everything must
happen *now*; that our worth is determined by our titles, our
achievements, and our productivity; and that we must be the
ones who keep the world spinning on its axis.

Today's Practice

Reflect on the following questions, using a journal or even
a sheet of paper. Think about the roles and responsibilities
you have in your family, at work, at school, at church, and
in your community. Where and how are you overextending
yourself? How do these patterns conform to or reinforce social hierarchies and patterns of oppression and exploitation?
What messages might you need to subvert in your context?

DAY 6

Self-Care Is Reparative

The LORD's word came to me: What do you mean by this proverb of yours about the land of Israel: "When parents eat unripe grapes, the children's teeth suffer"? As surely as I live, says the LORD God, no longer will you use this proverb in Israel!

EZEKIEL 18:1–3

"I woke up last night feeling a burden that was not mine. And I think it might belong to someone in this room," I announced to my 7:30 a.m. pastoral care class, sensing a heaviness in the air. Instead of launching into our planned discussion, we gathered in a circle and spent the entire class praying and weeping. By the end, the heaviness had lifted. That night I slept well.

Carrying other people's pain is an existential burden for people who identify as empaths, really, for anyone who tries to practice deep care and attention to the world around us. We are often so attuned to the feelings of others that we can experience their pain as if it were our own. The sorrows of the world weigh us down even when we don't know whose weight it is. In the words of Naughty by Nature, we're down with OPP . . . other people's pain. I know . . . I just dated myself.

Sometimes the other people whose pain we carry are no longer alive. We carry the trauma of our ancestors. Cutting-edge neuroscience and epigenetic research is showing us that violent trauma can change our biology, altering brain chemistry, neural structures, and even genetic expressions. Not only can these changes occur long after the traumatic situation has ended; they can also be transmitted across generations, passing from parent to child. Studies of Holocaust survivors, for example, have found that the effects can last for at least two generations. The grandchildren of Holocaust survivors show similar PTSD-related neuroendocrine changes as their grandparents, regardless of their own history of trauma and PTSD. What's more, these changes result in higher levels of problems such as hypertension, anxiety, and depression.[1]

Our bodies tell the stories of our ancestors' traumas: the Native Americans who were displaced, massacred, and sexually assaulted; the Africans who were kidnapped, shackled and transported across the ocean, enslaved, raped and beaten, and sold away from their families; the Jews who were imprisoned, brutalized, and murdered in concentration camps. Our bodies tell the stories of individual and cultural traumas: rape, physical abuse, immigration journeys and refugee camps, the 9/11 terrorist attacks, Native American boarding schools, Japanese American internment camps, school shootings, lynchings, deadly automobile accidents, police brutality, and race massacres in Tulsa, Wilmington, and Rosewood. Our bodies tell these stories of other people's pain without our even knowing them.

As a descendant of survivors of US chattel slavery, sharecropping, and Jim Crow, I practice self-care as a reparative strategy to heal pain and trauma that I have not directly experienced but that flows through my body in the form of elevated stress and inflammatory responses. I practice self-care to repair the story that my body has been told—that my ancestors' bodies were told—and to give it a new story. My ancestors were force-fed unripe grapes, but I do not have to suffer.

Today's Practice

Reflect on the following questions using a journal or sheet of paper: *What personal and family stories of trauma, violence, and abuse does your body tell? What generational traumas need healing?* You do not have to go into the details about the trauma. You do not even need to know what those details are. Perhaps you have only a vague feeling that *something* happened because you have seen the same effects play out in your family generation after generation. Just name those. Then pray for healing to take place in you and for your ancestors.

DAY 7

Self-Care
Is Sacred

Then God said, "Let us make humanity in our image
to resemble us so that they may take charge of the fish
of the sea, the birds in the sky, the livestock, all the
earth, and all the crawling things on earth." God created
humanity in God's own image, in the divine image God
created them, male and female God created them.

GENESIS 1:26–27

Week in Review

Getting serious about self-care begins with adjusting how we
have learned to think about ourselves and our care. Many of us

have internalized the idea that self-care means putting our wants ahead of the needs of other people or that it requires splurging on ourselves. This week, we have countered this view of self-care with one that is biblically and theologically rooted in the gift of our divine creation. Having been created in the likeness and image of God, our self is God's greatest gift to us. Repeatedly, scripture takes it as a given that we will care for ourselves. As the writer of Ephesians admonishes us, "No one ever hates his own body, but feeds it and takes care of it just like Christ does for the church because we are parts of his body" (Eph. 5:29–30).

When viewed in this light, we can think of self-care as the practices that help us to develop and nurture wholistic wellness as beings who are beautifully and wonderfully created by God in God's own image and likeness, and to sustain our vitality as agents of God's mission of justice, mercy, and peace in the world. Self-care is an act of faithful stewardship whereby we graciously and gratefully tend to the health and well-being of the divine gift that is our lives.

In a society built on a slaveholding economy in which every person's worth is determined by their productivity, prioritizing wellness is a subversive act. The practice of self-care in the pursuit of wellness is sacred. It resists the powers and principalities of a hyper-capitalist system. It reclaims the inherent dignity and worth that was bestowed on us at our creation. It proclaims the truth that God proclaimed about all of creation: that we are supremely good. We are sacred.

Silent Reflection

What is your reaction to thinking about self-care as a form of subversive stewardship? Where do you experience resistance to this idea? This might include internal resistance (such as feelings of guilt) or external obstacles (such as work and family responsibilities). How might you work with this resistance when it arises as you go through this book? What supports might you need to keep going over the next six weeks?

Prayer

God of creation, in whose image we are beautifully
and wonderfully made, teach us to embrace ourselves
with the same nurture and care with which you
tenderly sculpted us. Help us to overcome the barriers
and obstacles to sacred self-care that arise within and
beyond us. Strengthen us as we practice subversive
self-care. Empower us to cultivate caring and just
communities where all of your children know their
sacred worth and recognize it in others. Amen.

Hymn

STANDIN' IN THE NEED OF PRAYER
African American Heritage Hymnal, #441

Refrain:

It's me, it's me, O Lord,
Standin' in the need of prayer;
It's me, it's me, O Lord,
Standin' in the need of prayer.

Not my brother, not my sister, but it's me, O Lord,
Standin' in the need of prayer;
Not my brother, not my sister, but it's me, O Lord,
Standin' in the need of prayer.

Not the preacher, not the deacon, but it's me, O Lord.
Standin' in the need of prayer;
Not the preacher, not the deacon, but it's me, O Lord.
Standin' in the need of prayer.

Not my father, not my mother, but it's me, O Lord.
Standin' in the need of prayer;
Not my father, not my mother, but it's me, O Lord,
Standin' in the need of prayer.

Not the stranger, not my neighbor, but it's me, O Lord.
Standin' in the need of prayer;
Not the stranger, not my neighbor, but it's me, O Lord,
Standin' in the need of prayer.

Benediction

You have been reminded that you are God's good and perfect gift, created in the image of the Divine and endowed with sacred worth. May you go forth with the clarity and conviction that self-care is your right, your obligation, and your act of resistance. Amen.

WEEK 2

Mastering the Self-Care Fundamentals

In the first week, we addressed some of the myths and misconceptions about self-care. We defined self-care as the practices that help us to develop and nurture wholistic wellness as beings who are beautifully and wonderfully created by God in God's own image and likeness, and the practices that sustain our vitality as agents of God's mission of justice, mercy, and peace in the world. But what, exactly, does that look like? In week 2, we will further operationalize this definition by getting acquainted with the basics of self-care: the ways we nourish, hydrate, rest, and exert our bodies; the ways we honor our relationships and our emotions; and the ways we nurture our relationship with God.

DAY 8

Water to Live

Jesus answered, "Everyone who drinks this water will
be thirsty again, but whoever drinks from the water that
I will give will never be thirsty again. The water that I
give will become in those who drink it a spring of water
that bubbles up into eternal life."

JOHN 4:13–14

At its core, self-care is about attending to the body's day-to-day
needs. Last week, we explored how taking care of ourselves is
showing gratitude for the body God created for us by stewarding
that body well. This week is all about getting back to basics as to
how we do that for our physical bodies.

Most of us know that one of our body's most basic needs
is drinking water. The human body is made up of 60 percent

water, and the common advice from the medical community is that we need to drink sixty-four ounces of water each day. That should be simple, but in the US, we have an abundance of sweetened, bubbling, caffeinated, and alcoholic beverages that, quite frankly, taste better than plain water. Not to mention the fact that access to clean drinking water is becoming increasingly tenuous throughout the world, even in the wealthy US.

For the first twenty-five years of my life, I rarely drank water because I didn't like the way it tasted. When I was growing up, my family's standard beverages were apple juice, Kool-Aid, sweet tea, and lemonade. As an adult, I had to intentionally develop a taste for water. But even after I did, I usually didn't drink enough of it because I didn't want to be running to the bathroom all day, especially not in public spaces. At one job, the bathrooms were so unreliable that I avoided drinking during the entire workday. My doctor was not happy to hear that.

Today, there are varying opinions on how much water we need. Some experts still use the sixty-four-ounce guideline, while others say our water intake should be a percentage of our body weight. Some say that any fluid can count toward our daily intake (as long as it isn't diuretic), while some insist that only pure, non-sparkling water counts.

What everyone does agree on is that water, like air, is so vital to our existence that we cannot survive long without it. Perhaps that's why Jesus said that everyone who drinks water will thirst again. It wasn't that something was wrong with the water in that Samaritan well. Rather, he knew human bodies were created to need water so regularly that drinking it quenches us for only a short time. Jesus himself needed water and food every day.

That's why he was sitting at the well in the first place. Even the living water needed water to live!

Plus, the benefits of drinking water are many. In *Anticancer Living*, Lorenzo Cohen and Alison Jefferies describe water as "the flush button on all the toxins that build up in the digestive tract."[1] Water aids digestion by creating saliva and breaking down our food for its nutrients. It lubricates our joints and our skin. It is vital for brain function, protecting our brain and spinal cord, aiding in the production of hormones and neurotransmitters, and promoting cell growth and reproduction. It prevents kidney damage and regulates temperature and blood pressure. And it is water that transports the oxygen that we need throughout the body.

Very few of us would try to cut off or minimize our oxygen intake during the day, but we do the equivalent with water all the time. God created our bodies to need water. Let's give our bodies what they need.

Today's Practice

Hydrate your body well today. This might mean trying to drink water. If you don't usually drink at least sixty-four ounces during the day, it might mean aiming to drink sixty-four ounces of any kind of noncaffeinated, nonalcoholic beverage. There are some good (and free!) apps to help you track your daily water intake. Reflect on how you feel throughout the day with more hydration. And give yourself permission to go to the bathroom as often as needed in order to be well hydrated!

DAY 9

Our Daily Bread

Each individual should test himself or herself, and eat from the bread and drink from the cup in that way. Those who eat and drink without correctly understanding the body are eating and drinking their own judgment.

1 CORINTHIANS 11:28–29

Beyond air and water, food is our most basic need. Food is fuel. When I started driving, I used only Amoco gasoline. My grandfather insisted that Amoco was the best and that cars didn't run as well on any other brand. His zeal was successful in catechizing the rest of the family in the superiority of Amoco. For decades, we all used Amoco—and only Amoco—because we wanted our cars to run well. It was that simple.

But when it comes to fueling our bodies, there is so much conflicting information that we often hold conflicting sets of guidelines about food. Paleo. Keto. Gluten free. Vegan. Pescatarian. Atkins. Raw. Liquid. Intermittent fasting. There is no end to the number of diets that we have invented in our quest for weight control, disease management, and overall health. Every few months, it seems, we get new reports about what we are and are not supposed to eat. Is soy good for us or not? Are we eating too much protein or not enough? It's confusing, to say the least.

In addition, our busy lives mean that our food choices are often driven by convenience. We quickly grab whatever fills our stomach, costs little, and takes the least time to prepare and eat. If we have a history of trauma, financial insecurity, body shaming, or health issues, our relationship with food might be especially dysfunctional. In addition to eating to fill caloric needs, we may eat for emotional regulation. We need a different way to think about food.

Just as with our cars, self-care for our bodies means we need to give them the right kind of fuel. That means prioritizing nutrient-rich foods that maximize our physical well-being as well as avoiding foods that cause distress because they don't work for our body. To do that, we must know and understand our bodies well, as the writer of 1 Corinthians tells us. We have to listen to our bodies enough to know what we need to thrive. And we need to grant ourselves time: time to make meal plans, to shop for healthy foods, to cook, and even to sit down and eat in ways that aren't rushed (that includes eating meals with other people). When we take care of our physical body by fueling it well, we are setting ourselves up to better tackle whatever the day brings our way. The food we use to fuel our body can nourish and energize us, or it can hasten our path to breakdown.

Today's Practice

Make healthy eating choices for your body today. If you can, make time to prepare (or purchase, if need be) at least one healthy meal and to sit and eat it at a relaxed pace. If this is not a regular practice for you, consider what changes you might need to make in your life so that you can allot reasonable time to meet your body's most basic need.

DAY 10

Rest for Your Soul

It is pointless that you get up early and stay up late,
eating the bread of hard labor
because God gives sleep to those he loves.

PSALM 127:2

Steve Harvey once said, "Rich people don't sleep eight hours a day." There is a popular idea in our modern world that sleep is something to be minimized. For upwardly mobile people who are always trying to acquire and achieve more, sleeping may seem like a waste of time.

From the age of six, I had trouble going to and staying asleep. I spent years dodging daytime grogginess, napping at times to make up for lost nighttime sleep, drinking copious amounts of coffee and energy drinks during college and graduate school. I was low-key ashamed that I needed those elusive eight hours so badly. I wanted to be a person who could function with less sleep.

Rest and sleep are mentioned in scripture more than any other bodily need. After the creation of the world in Genesis, God rested. In the midst of the exodus from Egypt, God commanded the people of Israel to rest. The psalmist tells us that God gives sleep to those whom God loves, which is everyone. Jesus himself rested and slept. His sleep cycle was so strong that he could even sleep through a storm!

The reality is that none of us function well with less sleep; we just don't recognize the ways that it impacts us negatively, often until it is too late. I was forty when a new rheumatologist told me that getting a solid eight hours of sleep was the most important thing I could do to manage my fibromyalgia. But it wasn't until after my first breast cancer diagnosis, when I read Lorenzo Cohen and Alison Jefferies's book, *Anticancer Living*, that I got serious about regulating my sleep cycle.

Cohen and Jefferies reviewed a collection of well-designed studies demonstrating that getting fewer than eight hours of sleep per night contributes to poor health, including cancer, diabetes, heart disease, weight gain, and early-onset dementia and Alzheimer's disease. "Just forty minutes. That's all it takes for us to miss per night for our bodies to become vulnerable to a whole host of illness-related conditions."[1] It turns out that sleep isn't just about replenishing our physical energy. Research shows that our brain does some important work during—and only during—nighttime sleep. It cleans itself, flushing away neurotoxins that build up during the day.

This vital biological cycle means that it's more than pointless when we deprive our bodies of sleep; it is dangerous. Sleep is when our body restores itself. We all need to do the most we can to give our bodies the chance for restoration.

Today's Practice

Honor your sleep needs. Try to get at least seven hours of sleep tonight (which means being in bed for at least seven and a half hours, to give your body and mind a chance to wind down and fall asleep). Experiment with a wind-down routine, limiting your use of electronics at least an hour before bed and instead engaging in relaxing activities (aromatherapy, sipping herbal tea, reading). Minimize sources of outside and artificial light (I put duct tape over the lights on the cable boxes and power hubs). If sleep has been a long-standing problem for you, consider making an appointment with your physician or a sleep specialist to discuss it.

DAY 11

Moving for Good Health

Dear friend, I'm praying that all is well with you and that you enjoy good health in the same way that you prosper spiritually.

3 JOHN 1:2

I come from two athletic, sports-loving families. My dad played football in high school. My mother and grandmother were both basketball stars who might have had a good shot at the WNBA had it existed in their time. One uncle is a competitive bodybuilder in his fifties. And whether it's football, basketball, boxing, or track, sports talk dominates family gatherings on both sides.

Then there's me: utterly disinterested in sports, despite having studied or taught at some major sports schools. If the Hurricanes, Gators, Tar Heels, and Blue Devils couldn't turn me into a sports fan, it's just not happening.

For the first three decades of my life, I was not only disinterested in sports; I was inactive. I exercised only when required to, essentially during physical education classes and to lose weight for my wedding. Even then, my exertion was minimal. I was not trying to sweat out my short, permed hair for anybody's exercise.

In my thirties, I became more diligent about exercising and started running. But running caused me pain. When multiple physical therapists couldn't figure out the problem, I gave it up. Instead, I focused on the elliptical and on Pilates, yoga, and aerobic workouts, at one point working out for an hour six days per week. It took several years after my fibromyalgia diagnosis to realize that my exercise intensity was triggering flares. It was not that my activities were bad; they were just bad for me.

It was an odd dilemma. Movement is critical to health, including pain management and reducing cancer risk. Being sedentary for more than six hours per day is not only associated with increased mortality from some cancers; it's also associated with developing insulin resistance, heart disease, immune deficiency, depression, and cognitive decline. Taking care of our bodies means giving them physical activity. But moving too much or in the wrong way triggered painful flares. I had gone from one extreme to the other.

After a few years of trial and error, I found the right activities for my body: low-impact cardio, swimming, walking, and yin yoga. I learned to balance the long periods of sitting required by my work with regular bouts of activity during the day, including the occasional midday dance break!

Like spiritual prosperity, good health is not about perfection. It doesn't require being disease free or maintaining the perfect weight. Rather, it is about maximizing our wellness given the realities of our lives, including our physical limitations. It is about learning how to find the right type and amount of activity that work for us.

Today's Practice

Move your body in ways that challenge and restore you. Maybe this means leveling up your existing routine or trying something new. Or maybe you just need to start small and celebrate some wins. Take a walk around your neighborhood. Choose the stairs instead of the elevator. Do ten minutes of light stretching. Whatever you do, find some way to be active today.

With All Your Mind and Soul

In the same way, the Spirit comes to help our weakness.
We don't know what we should pray, but the Spirit
himself pleads our case with unexpressed groans.
The one who searches hearts knows how the Spirit
thinks, because he pleads for the saints, consistent
with God's will.

ROMANS 8:26–27

I am a cognitive time traveler. I spend a lot of time living in
an imagined future, planning ahead. I am constantly thinking
about what I want and need to do, whether it's later today or
later this year. I think about what is likely to happen and how

I might prepare for it. I even think about what other people or institutions could do to improve themselves.

I also spend a lot of time living in the past, ruminating. It is a downside of being self-reflective. I rehearse old stories, reliving them in my head. I think about what happened, what I could have done differently, how it turned out, what I learned from it. Sometimes it is useful; often, though, it is not.

Living *out of time* in these ways can be an obstacle to attending to the self-care practices that my body-mind-spirit needs *today*. For this reason, mindfulness practices such as meditation have become the anchor for my self-care practices. Meditation grounds me in the present, inviting me to attend to what is happening right now: the thoughts, emotions, and bodily sensations I am experiencing. Mindfulness helps me to be aware of what I need by drawing my attention to what is. Is there pain in the body? Fatigue? Am I feeling anxious? Lonely? Mindfulness is not just about the mind, though we will explore this in more detail in week 6. It could just as easily be called *bodyfulness* or *heartfulness*.

Meditation allows me to connect with myself, and it also allows me to connect with Spirit. Each time I sit at my meditation altar, I do so with the expectation that God is in the stillness. When I settle on the breath as my anchor, I am focusing on the very life force that God breathed into me and all of humanity. When I sit in silence, I acknowledge the limitation of human language to connect with the Divine. I invite the Spirit herself to plead the needs that I cannot even fathom, and I allow space for the Divine to speak back to me.

Some days I hear something; most days I do not, other than the longings and anxieties of my own heart. But that, too, is holy.

Today's Practice

Be deliberate in setting aside time for meditation, prayer, or devotional reading (see day 41 for some ideas of different forms of this). If you want to start a meditation practice, begin with a five-minute breath awareness practice and build from there (see the self-care resource guide on my website, www.drchanequa.com). If you're an experienced meditator, you may need to regulate or ritualize your practice, designating a place in your home for a practice space, setting aside a specific time for meditation, or reinvigorating your practice through group sits and retreats.

DAY 13

The Healing Power of Relationship

Two are better than one because they have a good return for their hard work. If either should fall, one can pick up the other. But how miserable are those who fall and don't have a companion to help them up! Also, if two lie down together, they can stay warm. But how can anyone stay warm alone? Also, one can be overpowered, but two together can put up resistance. A three-ply cord doesn't easily snap.

ECCLESIASTES 4:9–12

Relationships are critical to who we are as human beings. We are not just selves; we are selves-in-relationship. Our identities and personalities are created through our connections to other people, first our family and caregivers, later our friends and romantic partners. In the wisdom literature, scripture repeatedly tells us of the value of family and friends. The writer of Ecclesiastes tells us that "two are better than one because they have a good return for their hard work" (Eccles. 4:9), and Proverbs tells us, "friends love all the time, and kinsfolk are born for times of trouble" (Prov. 17:17).

Restorative relationships are based upon mutuality and reciprocity, authenticity, and vulnerability. In them, we are seen, affirmed, challenged, and loved. They sustain us and encourage us to care for ourselves. Unfortunately, restorative relationships are not the bulk of our interactions. Many of our relationships are transactional or obligatory, especially in the workforce but sometimes also in our families and friendships. They may be enjoyable but mostly one-directional, with us doing most of the giving. When others fall, we are there to pick them up. But when we fall, there's no one to help us. These relationships can be parasitic, sucking up our energy in harmful ways.

Sometimes our Christian identity is the barrier to forming and maintaining healthy relationships. Some people think that a good Christ follower doesn't need other people. "As long as I got King Jesus, I don't need nobody else." Or sometimes we stay in relationship with people who are not good for us because we think it's our duty. Very often, time is the culprit, our busy lives and frantic pace preventing us from taking the time to nurture relationships with people who replenish us and whom we replenish in return.

One Friday night a few years ago, I met a cousin for dinner.

After a week of work, I was exhausted and wanted to just go home and collapse into bed. But we had been looking forward to this for a long time, and it had been difficult to coordinate our busy schedules. Over the next few hours, we laughed and commiserated and held space for each other. By the time we parted, the fatigue had vanished and I felt rejuvenated, not just for that evening but for days afterward.

That's the power of dwelling in restorative relationship: it revives, renews, and restores us.

Today's Practice

Be intentional today about connecting with someone who replenishes you (and ideally who you also replenish). This could mean picking up the phone and calling someone, as opposed to texting, or even visiting with someone in person. But it could also be deliberately nurturing relationships with the people with whom you share life on a daily basis: playing a board game with your family, sitting for coffee with a roommate, going to lunch with a friend or colleague, calling someone you haven't seen in a long time, or making a dinner date with a friend or relative whose company revives and replenishes you.

Good Self-Care Shepherds

The LORD is my shepherd.
I lack nothing.
He lets me rest in grassy meadows;
he leads me to restful waters;
he keeps me alive.
He guides me in proper paths
for the sake of his good name.
Even when I walk
through the darkest valley,
I fear no danger because you are with me.
Your rod and your staff—
they protect me.
You set a table for me
right in front of my enemies.
You bathe my head in oil;

my cup is so full it spills over!

Yes, goodness and faithful love

will pursue me all the days of my life,

and I will live in the LORD's house

as long as I live.

PSALM 23

Week in Review

Staying hydrated. Eating right for our bodies. Maintaining good rhythms of rest and activity. Engaging in prayer and meditation. Enjoying restorative relationships. The basic practices of self-care are simple yet often difficult to practice consistently. They are especially difficult for Christians who have been taught that our bodies are sinful and that the point of discipleship is to subdue our "natural" self so that our "spiritual" self can flourish. Many of us are further disconnected from our bodies through the patriarchal, ableist, and Eurocentric messages that society gives us about what an ideal body looks like (we'll return to this theme on several occasions over the next few weeks).

But our bodies are not just the housing for our spirits and our minds. We are fully embodied beings who can experience the world only through our body-mind-spirit. Caring for ourselves requires us to embrace our embodiment and the needs that come along with it, in the same way that God cares for us as embodied people.

Scripture yields plenty of evidence that God is deeply con-

cerned with our health and well-being, that is, with our embodiment. Psalm 23 reveals God as the good shepherd who desires
for us to feed in good pasture, to rest in safety and peace, to
be surrounded by love, to have cups that overflow with good
drink, and even to anoint our bodies with perfume and oil. God
is the good shepherd because God cares for our physical needs,
our emotional needs, even our relational needs. Caring for our
embodied selves, then, is our birthright (or, better yet, our
"creation right"). It is good, in and of itself, because through
it we extend the same love to ourselves that God gives to us.
Self-care also sustains our vitality as agents of God's mission
of justice, mercy, and peace in the world by developing and
nurturing our embodied selves.

Good self-care requires three things: self-awareness, intentionality, and flexibility. That is, we must know our body-mind-spirit
well enough to identify what we need; we must be deliberate and
intentional about structuring our lives to allow for self-care; and
we must be flexible enough to adapt as our needs and circumstances change. But it all starts with learning what we need.
It starts with learning to be good shepherds of our embodied
selves.

Silent Reflection

What are your basic self-care needs? That is, what basic self-care
practices do you need to observe each day or week in order to
be as healthy as your body allows? Be sure to consider nutrition,
physical activity, rest, relationships, and spirituality. If you have

any chronic or serious health issues, include the practices that help you to manage them. Don't worry about setting goals yet in terms of frequency and length. First, just think about what you need. If you'd like to go deeper, use the Sacred Self-Care Inventory in the back of this book to assess your current practices and needs.

Prayer

God our sustainer, you have revealed yourself to us as one who cares for us as a shepherd cares for their flock. From providing manna in the desert to multiplying loaves and fishes, you have taught us that caring for our bodily needs is holy. Help us to honor our creation as embodied beings by shepherding ourselves with the same love and care. Give us the wisdom to recognize our true needs, the provisions we need to fulfill them, and the steadfastness to overcome obstacles to caring for ourselves. Remind us that we are worthy of care, and empower us to cultivate communities of mutual care and affection. Amen.

Hymn

THE LORD IS MY SHEPHERD
African American Heritage Hymnal, #426

The Lord is my shepherd, no want shall I know;
I feed in green pastures, safe-folded I rest;
He leadeth my soul where the still waters flow;
Restores me when wand'ring, redeems when oppressed,
Restores me when wand'ring, redeems when oppressed.
Through the valley and shadow of death though I stray,
Since Thou art my Guardian, no evil I fear;
Thy rod shall defend me, Thy staff be my stay;
No harm can befall, with my Comforter near,
No harm can befall, with my Comforter near.
In the midst of affliction my table is spread;
With blessings unmeasured my cup runneth o'er;
With perfume and oil Thou anointest my head;
O what shall I ask of Thy providence more?
O what shall I ask of Thy providence more?
Let goodness and mercy, my bountiful God,
Still follow my steps till I meet Thee above.
I seek by the path which my ancestors trod,
Through the land of their sojourn, Thy kingdom of love;
Through the land of their sojourn, Thy kingdom of love.

Benediction

You have been reminded that God is the Good Shepherd who is
intimately concerned for your health and well-being. May you go
forth with the wisdom to know your needs and the conviction
that caring for yourself is holy. Amen.

WEEK 3

Practicing Self-Compassion

If self-care is so simple, why is it so hard to commit to it? Even when we know we need care, we struggle to practice it consistently. It is not that we think self-care is unimportant; rather, we think it is not *as* important as other activities, especially those that directly benefit the people in our lives or the institutions we are a part of. In other words, we think that we are less important than other people and institutions and that caring for ourselves is an impediment to caring for others. Maintaining good self-care, then, requires loving ourselves enough to dedicate our time and energy to caring for ourselves. It requires cultivating self-compassion, which we will turn to over the course of this week.

As You Love Your Neighbor

He responded, *"You must love the Lord your God with all your heart, with all your being, with all your strength, and with all your mind, and love your neighbor as yourself."*

LUKE 10:27

Caring for ourselves is not just about what we *do* for ourselves. It is also about how we *feel and think* about ourselves. Scripture urges us not to think of ourselves too highly, to avoid the sin of pride, and to embrace the virtue of humility. In much of the Christian tradition, we have taken these teachings to an extreme. Many of us—especially women—have learned that not only should we not think of ourselves too highly; we shouldn't think of ourselves at all!

Jesus had something different to say: you must love your neighbor as you love yourself. In childhood, many of us learned this as the *golden rule*, the principle that we should treat others as we wish to be treated. The idea is so compelling that there's some version of the golden rule in nearly every major religion and across many of the world's cultures. Jesus ratchets it up a notch, teaching us that loving God and loving our neighbors as ourselves is more than a good idea; it is the greatest of all the divine laws, the Great Commandment. In Luke, Jesus follows this statement with the parable of the Good Samaritan to show us how self-love and neighbor love work together.

The parable of the Good Samaritan is about *compassion*, which, translated literally, means "to suffer with." Compassion allows us to connect to the feelings of others, to respond to their suffering with feelings of kindness, and to desire that their suffering be ameliorated. Compassion also guides us to interact with other people in ways that do not cause them pain and suffering.

While many of us do that already, we struggle with extending that same kind of compassion to ourselves. Think about it: if we were to treat other people as we treat ourselves, that might look less like kindness and more like heaping constant judgment and criticism upon them, burdening them with excessive responsibility, using demeaning language toward them, and demanding that they neglect their own health.

Self-care requires self-compassion, that is, treating ourselves with kindness, comfort, empathy, and understanding. When we practice self-compassion, we recognize our own suffering (including the suffering we inflict on ourselves, which can take the form of self-judgment and criticism) and we are compelled to alleviate it. Self-compassion is self-care turned inward. It is not only changing our behaviors toward ourselves but also changing our thoughts and feelings about ourselves.

Today's Practice

Exercise self-compassion in at least one meaningful way today. This could include the following:

- Giving yourself a compliment
- Taking a break during your day instead of working nonstop
- Forgiving yourself if you make a mistake
- Reminding yourself that you're doing the best you can and being patient with yourself if you feel overwhelmed
- Allowing difficult emotions and bodily sensations to exist without judging or shaming yourself for them

Consider journaling about what you did and how it felt. Pay attention to any resistance that you felt about showing yourself compassion.

DAY 16

Watch Your Words

No one can tame the tongue, though. It is a restless evil, full of deadly poison. With it we both bless the Lord and Father and curse human beings made in God's likeness. Blessing and cursing come from the same mouth. My brothers and sisters, it just shouldn't be this way!

JAMES 3:8–10

Humans are the only species God gifted with complex capacities for language. We can speak, write, and think using words. We can develop new words and change the meaning of existing words. Like the Word of God, human language has creative power. We use words to form and maintain relationships, to build and sustain institutions, to establish the laws that organize societies.

Unfortunately, the power of our words is not just generative. Words have destructive and oppressive capacities as well. We use words to wage wars, to break spirits, and to establish unjust laws that enslave and oppress. Some of the harshest words are not those that we speak aloud or put in writing for other people to hear or read. They are our self-talk, the words that exist mainly in our head, the inner dialogue that we have with ourselves about ourselves.

My self-talk often comes in the form of *should* messages: the things that I should do, the rules I must follow, even the relationships that I have to maintain in order to be a good person—a good mother, wife, daughter, professor, and Christian. Some of these messages come from external sources: family, teachers and mentors, colleagues and employers, church, and society at large. Others, though, I have created, often unintentionally and unconsciously. These messages are rarely true, and they set unrealistically high bars by which I judge myself. They rob me of my freedom to choose and tempt me to live beyond my limitations. They are enemies to self-care and self-compassion.

Should messages are hard to control and are often buried within our consciousness. What we can do, though, is be aware of how they work. Nearly every morning, for example, my self-talk tells me that I *should* shorten or skip praying, meditating, and exercising because I *need* to get to work sooner. The thing is, that is not true. Since I have some flexibility in my schedule and whether I work from home, my internal idea about what time I *have* to be at work is just that—my idea, not a rule. Perhaps more important is the implicit message behind my self-talk: work (and pleasing people at work) is more important than my health. Fortunately, I am learning to recognize that self-talk, acknowledge the need behind it, and gently tell it to shut up.

James is right: no one can tame the tongue. But it doesn't have to be this way. We can try to unearth these self-defeating messages from their hiding places and become familiar with them so that we are more likely to recognize them when they appear. We can respond to ourselves with compassion rather than condemnation. We can use the power of our words to bless ourselves as humans made in God's likeness.

Today's Practice

Pay attention to your self-talk today, especially the internal beliefs and messages about what you should, must, ought to, need to, or have to do. How do these messages affect your well-being? How do they make you feel? Are there any themes that rise to the surface often? Where do they impede self-care?

Befriend Your Inner Critic

Love is patient, love is kind, it isn't jealous, it doesn't brag, it isn't arrogant, it isn't rude, it doesn't seek its own advantage, it isn't irritable, it doesn't keep a record of complaints.

1 CORINTHIANS 13:4–5

I used to love to hear my maternal grandmother tell family stories. She had no shortage of tales about the shenanigans of her eight children. But one of the stories she told was about me. I was staying with her and my grandfather when I was about five or six. Granddaddy had been outside changing the oil in his car when I came running outside, excited to show him something. "Stop!" he yelled, bringing my excitement and motion to a standstill. He didn't want me outside because he had spilled oil on the driveway. I nodded silently and turned back into the house. A few days later, Grandmama realized that I had been uncharacteristically quiet. "Baby, what's wrong with you?" I immediately burst into tears. "Grandaddy yelled at me!" My grandfather felt horrible and resolved to never yell at me again.

Even at that early age, I was deeply invested in being a good girl who pleased others. I was already a budding perfectionist. As long as I can remember, I have had much higher ideals and expectations for myself than I have for other people. Even as a kid, I judged myself mercilessly for limitations and mistakes. Consequently, I was sensitive to anything resembling criticism, even a cautionary "Stop!" meant to protect me from an oil spill.

I still have a very vocal inner critic bombarding me with messages about not being good enough and not doing enough. Similar to the *should* messages that set unrealistic expectations for ourselves, self-criticism is another form of self-talk, one that berates us for not meeting those expectations. My inner critic is especially sneaky because it often poses as self-awareness, pointing out my flaws and telling me that I can and should do better. It also poses as humility, preventing me from fully celebrating myself and my achievements lest I think too highly of myself. It often stops me in my tracks, limiting me from pursuing opportunities or ideas that seem too big for someone as insignificant as me.

Self-compassion is the antidote to self-criticism. In her book *Self-Compassion*, Kristin Neff says, "The best way to counteract self-criticism . . . is to understand it, have compassion for it, and then replace it with a kinder response."[1] I have been working at befriending my inner critic, trying to understand her voice and her motives. It turns out that her messages of limitation, inadequacy, and fear are motivated by love and meant to shield me from disappointment, rejection, and pain. Slowly, I am trying to teach her a different love language, one that is patient, that is kind, and that doesn't keep a record of complaints.

Today's Practice

Pay attention to your self-talk again. This time, notice the voice of your inner critic or saboteur. How do you experience it? What does it say? What is its tone? How does it make you feel? Who, if anyone, does it resemble? What might it be trying to accomplish? Take your time with these reflections. You might spend some time journaling about them. You might even draw a picture of your inner critic. Don't worry about your drawing skills. No one is going to see it but you.

Affirm Your Enoughness

We all make mistakes often, but those who don't make mistakes with their words have reached full maturity. Like a bridled horse, they can control themselves entirely. When we bridle horses and put bits in their mouths to lead them wherever we want, we can control their whole bodies.

JAMES 3:2–3

Self-talk can tear us down with messages of judgment, criticism, and fear. But our self-talk can build us up, too. Like bits placed in horses' mouths to lead them, the words in our mouths, minds, and hearts can lead us away from self-neglect and toward self-compassion.

One way to tap into the positive power of self-talk is to use affirmations. Now, I admit that I cringe at affirmations that imply that we can control our experiences simply by thinking positively, as if evil and oppression aren't real. But affirmations can be a powerful form of corrective self-talk. They can help to replace negative messages that we've been giving ourselves or that we've heard from others. They can reinforce our deepest values, including our commitments to health and well-being. That is important because we live in a world that constantly tries to convince us that we are insufficient, unworthy, and incapable.

As someone socialized into the myth of the StrongBlack-Woman, I learned that my worth depended upon putting the needs of other people and institutions ahead of my own.[1] As an academic and minister, I have been trained to value myself on the basis of my usefulness and productivity. Then there are the messages learned about what it means to be a good mother, wife, and daughter. It is relentless. It is hard to be compassionate toward yourself when you always think you're missing the mark on service and efficiency.

When I began my self-care journey twenty years ago, I started each day by repeating a set of affirmations. The set has changed over time, but there's one I return to frequently: *I am enough.*

I am enough turns out to be the message that I need most often to tame my inner critic, who unfortunately tries to prepare me for the world by reiterating its messages that I am not a good enough mother, partner, daughter, teacher, scholar, minister, or Christian. My inner critic constantly dangles in front of me what I should, ought, and must do in order to feel good enough. But it's a trick. Because when I do that thing, the feeling is fleeting.

I am enough, in contrast, is not a feeling. It's a *knowing*, one that comes from deep within my fiber. In this world that profits from our not-enoughness, I often have to remind myself of the worth and value that God affirmed in me and all of creation when "God saw everything he had made: it was supremely good" (Gen. 1:31).

Today's Practice

Think back to what you have noticed about your self-talk this week. What messages have you received from your inner critic? How might you reframe those messages to practice more kindness and compassion toward yourself? Imagine, for example, that your inner critic becomes your inner cheerleader. What messages do you need to hear from your inner cheerleader? Consider turning these into affirmations. If it feels right, start with *I am enough*.

DAY 19

Moving Beyond Self-Judgment

In every way, then, speak and act as people who will be judged by the law of freedom. There will be no mercy in judgment for anyone who hasn't shown mercy. Mercy overrules judgment.

JAMES 2:12–13

"She does not have the body to wear that."

The thought appeared like an unwelcome guest as I watched the woman walk across the parking lot in a tight-fitting outfit. It had become a reflexive action—appraising the body of every woman that I saw. But that day, my judgmental and unkind thought brought me to a mental standstill. Where did I get the idea that women's bodies should come in a particular shape?

How had I arrived at this point of making every woman I saw an unwilling participant in my internal beauty contest?

It was the age of the music video. Being in my late twenties and childless, I spent a lot of time watching music television. From *Video Soul* to *MTV Jams* to *106 & Park*, videos were the main meal in my television appetite, whether I actively watched or had them playing in the background as I analyzed my dissertation data and read for classes. By the late 1990s, the video vixen dominated hip-hop's portrayal of women, with scantily clad, gyrating bodies birthed by the lyrics of the Commodores' song "Brick House." It was a lot of time being bombarded with images of bodies that were often surgically sculpted to meet cishet men's unrealistic 36-24-36 fantasies (cishet refers to people who are both cisgender and heterosexual).

I had accepted that standard and routinely judged women's bodies against it, including my own. While my inner critic was generally vocal about my self-perceived shortcomings, she was unrelenting when it came to my body. I had internalized so much criticism about my body that I readily turned the judgment toward others. Every harsh critique that I uttered or thought about another woman's body was a reflection of the hostility that I felt toward my own.

Just a few years earlier, I had given up the war with my hair, going natural after two decades of trying to force my hair to conform to the silky straight locks ideal of a Eurocentric society. That afternoon, I decided it was time to call off the war with my body, to embrace my round belly, full hips, and big thighs. I needed a way to unlearn body judgment and to counter it with body acceptance. Each time that I caught myself negatively judging another woman's appearance, I said to myself: "She is created in the image of God, and so am I."

James's epistle exhorts us to "speak and act as people who will be judged by the law of freedom," letting mercy override judgment (James 2:12–13). Often, our inability to speak mercy toward others is rooted in our inability to do it for ourselves. We judge others with the same harsh measure with which we judge ourselves. Freedom comes in learning to accept and love ourselves for who we are now, treating ourselves with the mercy and compassion that Christ embodied. When we allow self-compassion to overrule self-judgment, our cup of compassion overflows, and we respond to others out of that overflow.

Today's Practice

Continue monitoring your self-talk and, today especially, your thoughts about your body. When you notice that you are judging yourself, repeat this affirmation inspired by Psalm 139: *I am beautifully and wonderfully made in the image of God.* To take this practice deeper, repeat the affirmation to yourself while looking at yourself unclothed in a full-length mirror.

DAY 20

Spreading Self-Compassion

May the Lord cause you to increase and enrich your love for each other and for everyone in the same way as we also love you. May the love cause your hearts to be strengthened, to be blameless in holiness before our God and Father when our Lord Jesus comes with all his people. Amen.

1 THESSALONIANS 3:12–13

A strange thing happened when I became intentional about caring for myself: I began to care more for other people. Instead of rushing out of the office after being deskbound all day, I took time during the day to check in with colleagues. Many of them seemed surprised that someone would stop by their office with no agenda! It wasn't just at work, either. I quickly noticed a change in my relationships with friends and family. I became more deliberate about calling my relatives and spending time with friends. That might seem unremarkable to extroverts, but my fellow introverts can understand how I was slightly weirded out by my newfound interest in socializing!

It turns out that self-compassion is self-propagating. When we begin to genuinely love and care for ourselves as an act of gratitude to the God who created us, our self-compassion overflows and naturally spreads to the world around us. We grow closer to who God created us to be: loving human beings who were made for relationship with God and with one another. Before long, not only do we want to connect more deeply to others, but we also want them to experience the same benefits of self-care. And we do not want our self-care to be at their expense.

Genuine self-compassion is deeply relational. The more I exercise self-compassion—by recognizing and accepting my limits, by setting realistic expectations for myself, by forgiving myself for my mistakes and shortcomings, by refraining from harsh self-criticism—the greater compassion I develop toward others and the more I want for them what I want for myself: health, vitality, and joy.

The opposite is true, too. As we learned yesterday, self-judgment is contagious. If my colleagues have a lot of *should* language, we will all be pressured to take on more work than necessary. If my students are impatient and unforgiving toward themselves as they learn new material, they're not likely to extend much grace to me when I fall behind in grading. If my senior pastor thinks that she can and should do it all, she's going to expect the same thing of her ministry team. And because I'm a pleaser, their *should* language is going to trigger my *should* language, and before you know it, we'll all be spiraling toward burnout together. In each case, my capacity for self-compassion will be constrained by the capacities of the people who surround me.

The good news is that self-compassion is contagious, too. It is like the love of God that Paul describes in 1 Thessalonians, increasing and enriching our love for one another.

Today's Practice

Look for an opportunity to be a self-care ambassador today by encouraging another person to exercise self-compassion. For example, you might do the following:

- Acknowledge a person's right to feel sad, angry, or anxious if they're going through a difficult time
- Encourage a person to be gentle with themselves when they lapse into self-judgment
- Remind someone to be patient with themselves when they are learning something new
- Help people identify false *should* messages that might be contributing to their stress

DAY 21

Compassion Turned Inward

One of the legal experts heard their dispute and saw how well Jesus answered them. He came over and asked him, "Which commandment is the most important of all?" Jesus replied, "The most important one is *Israel, listen! Our God is the one Lord, and you must love the Lord your God with all your heart, with all your being, with all your mind, and with all your strength.* The second is this, *You will love your neighbor as yourself.* No other commandment is greater than these."

MARK 12:28–31

Week in Review

There can be no self-care without self-compassion, which is compassion turned inward. It is the ability to connect to our feelings, to respond to our suffering with kindness, and to desire that our suffering be ameliorated. Self-compassion prompts us to treat ourselves in ways that alleviate, rather than cause or amplify, our pain and suffering. While many Christians understand compassion, mercy, and kindness to be essential in our interactions with others, we don't always see these as core values for our relationship with ourselves. We neglect our self-care, directly and indirectly contributing to our pain and suffering. We judge ourselves for our own suffering, listening to the voice of our inner critic as it rehearses our shortcomings, our errors, and our deficiencies. As James teaches us, it doesn't have to be this way (James 3:10).

Implicit in Jesus's commandment to love our neighbors as ourselves is the assumption that we are *supposed* to love ourselves. We are supposed to be kind and gentle, caring and nurturing, empowering and forgiving of ourselves. If we are unable to do this, ultimately we may be unable to do it for our neighbors. And if we cannot love our neighbors, whom we can see, we cannot love God, whom we cannot see (1 John 4:20). Self-compassion, then, is not indulgence; it is a necessity for true discipleship.

Silent Reflection

What did you learn about yourself in paying attention to your self-talk this week? How vocal is your inner critic, and what messages does it send? In what ways do you affirm and encourage yourself? Consider identifying a core set of three to five affirmations to repeat to yourself daily. Print or write them in places that are visible to you throughout your day as reminders to practice love and kindness toward yourself. You can also use the affirmation meditation in the self-care resource guide on my website, www.drchanequa.com.

Prayer

God of compassion, who cares for us with the tender love of a mother nursing her young, help us to care for ourselves with the same mercy and gentleness that you offer us. Help us to speak words of maturity, wisdom, and kindness toward ourselves. Let our cup so overflow with self-love that we spread it to others, encouraging them to love themselves as your divine image bearers. Amen.

Hymn

GOD WILL TAKE CARE OF YOU
African American Heritage Hymnal, #137

Refrain:
God will take care of you,
Through ev'ry day,

O'er all the way;
He will take care of you,
God will take care of you.

Be not dismayed whate'er betide,
God will take care of you;
Beneath His wings of love abide,
God will take care of you.
Through days of toil when heart does fail,
God will take care of you;
When dangers fierce your path assail,
God will take care of you.
All you may need He will provide,
God will take care of you;
Nothing you ask will be denied,
God will take care of you.
No matter what may be the test,
God will take care of you;
Lean, weary one, upon His breast,
God will take care of you.

Benediction

You have been reminded that you were created by God, whose love and mercy know no end, who spoke creation into existence, and who has given you the power of love in both word and deed. May you be so filled with compassion and love for yourself that it overflows and touches all with whom you come into contact. Amen.

WEEK 4

Setting Healthy Boundaries

Whether it is for ourselves or others, caring requires compassion. But what about the other part of self-care—the self? What if a person lacks a sense of self? That is often the case for those of us who have been socialized to care for the needs of others at the expense of our own. We can be so other-focused that we never develop an authentic identity, or we struggle to maintain that identity in the face of life's pressures. In this week, then, we focus on the best tool for establishing and maintaining a self to care for—boundaries. As we'll see, boundaries are both emotional and relational forms of self-care.

No Boundaries, No Self-Care

We won't take pride in anything more than what is appropriate. Let's look at the boundaries of our work area that God has assigned to us. It's an area that includes you. We aren't going out of bounds, as if our work area doesn't extend as far as you. We were the first ones to travel as far as Corinth with the gospel of Christ. We don't take pride in what other people do outside of our boundaries. We hope that our work will be extended even more by you as your faith grows, until it expands fully (within the boundaries, of course).

2 CORINTHIANS 10:13–15

When someone suggests that self-care is selfish or asks whether it is, it is a telltale sign that the person lacks a healthy sense of self.

Self-care begins with self-differentiation, the establishment of an identity that is distinct from our family and our peers. Psychologist Erik Erikson's stage theory of psychosocial development states that identity formation is the central crisis of the adolescent years.[1] Adolescence is filled with so much angst because we are trying to figure out who we are versus who our parents, families, and churches want us to be. In Erikson's theory, we successfully achieve the goal of self-differentiation when we develop an authentic identity that is informed by, yet distinct from, our families of origin.

In truth, self-differentiation does not end in adolescence. For most of us, it is a lifelong process of discovering, becoming, and acting in congruence with our authentic selves. Self-differentiation is an ongoing process of affirming *This is who I am* and *This is who I am not*.

Boundaries are the imaginary walls that define who we are and who we are not. They establish, define, and safeguard our personhood by delineating what we will and will not do, allow, practice, or accept. Good boundaries are clear, flexible, and porous. They honor our needs, desires, and limits. They determine who gets access to us and how much access they get. Boundaries are like the movable walls in a big conference center or banquet hall. Depending upon the circumstances, we can configure them differently. Activities allowed in one part may be off-limits in others. And not everyone gets access to the same spaces.

Healthy boundaries allow us to meet our own needs while being in relationship with other people. When we lack boundaries, we yield control over ourselves to other people. They set the limits, which means they can give us less than we need from the relationship or they can demand more from us than we are capable of giving. On the other hand, when we have excessively rigid boundaries, we guard and control ourselves so tightly that we are closed off to the possibility of new self-discovery and we lack meaningful relationships with others.

Boundaries are how God created the world, differentiating the earth from the heavens, the land from the sky and the waters, and creatures from one another. In Genesis, the first act of human sin is essentially a boundary violation! And much of scripture, from the Ten Commandments to the Sermon on the Mount, describes God establishing—and, in Jesus, modeling— the rules and principles that differentiate the people of God. Setting and honoring boundaries, then, is good, necessary, and holy work.

Today's Practice

Reflect on the following questions, using a journal or a sheet of paper: Who or what is in control of your boundaries, making the decisions about how you are configured and accessed? Do particular people or situations make it more difficult for you to establish and maintain healthy boundaries? Think about the relationships or situations in which you repeatedly feel stressed, overwhelmed, overcommitted, or taken advantage of. This might be with family and friends, but it could also be with work, church, or volunteer positions.

DAY 23

Good Boundary Lines

The boundary lines have fallen for me in pleasant places;
I have a goodly heritage.

PSALM 16:6 (NRSV)

Boundaries would be easier to set and maintain if they were the same for everyone. Then there would never be any boundary violations because we would all know what to do and not to do. Boundaries, though, are highly individualized. What works for one person does not work for another. And even for one individual, boundaries are not fixed rules. They are fluid, changing across time, circumstance, and relationship.

Since boundaries are neither visible nor universally agreed upon, they exist only if we state them. When people cross them, we have to let them know. Many boundary violations happen because the other person does not know what our boundaries are. They may have different boundaries, or we may not have communicated ours clearly and consistently. We may be expecting them to read our minds or to do our boundary-building work for us.

Maybe in the future, we'll have some fancy biotech that alerts other people about our capabilities and limits. Before asking us to do something, people will open an app, tap on our avatar, and get a message like "That function is not available at this time." Until then, maintaining boundaries requires us to put in some work.

There are four basic steps in setting boundaries. First, we determine the type of boundary we need. This requires knowing ourselves enough to know our needs. Second, we directly and clearly communicate the boundary to others. Third, we follow up the boundary setting with action. This means we should not violate our own boundaries, and we have to let other people know when they do . . . every single time. There is no "set it and forget it." We may have to set some boundaries daily, even multiple times each day.

Finally, we have to manage the discomfort we feel when we hold firm to our boundaries. For many of us, this includes anxiety about whether we are disappointing others and how the relationship will be impacted. We may worry about losing the relationship or future opportunities. If we don't manage this discomfort, it becomes the biggest boundary violator of all. It is not pleasant, but working through it is how we set good boundaries.

Sometimes good boundary lines just fall in pleasant places (Ps. 16:6, NRSV). But often, they are constructed through our hard work. The good news is that as cocreators with God, we have the capacity to create our own boundaries (1 Cor. 3:9).

Today's Practice

Identify one boundary that you would like to set and maintain today. How will you communicate that boundary and to whom? What is likely to challenge the boundary? What actions will you take to protect it? Identify a kind but firm way that you can state the boundary to others (doing so ahead of time can help communicating your boundary to others go smoother).

DAY 24

Honor Your Limits

When someone says, "I belong to Paul," and someone
else says, "I belong to Apollos," aren't you acting like
people without the Spirit? After all, what is Apollos?
What is Paul? They are servants who helped you to
believe. Each one had a role given to them by the Lord:
I planted, Apollos watered, but God made it grow.

1 CORINTHIANS 3:4–6

Boundary violations sometimes occur because people intentionally intrude upon them. But most of the time, they occur
because we take on too much.

Having too much on our figurative plate is a telltale sign of
having boundary issues. When we have trouble maintaining
healthy boundaries, we take on tasks, roles, and responsibilities
that are not our own. We are unaware of our priorities, needs,

and obligations, and we frequently exceed our load-bearing capacities. Without a clear sense of self, we look to other people and institutions to define and validate us. And as Paul's words to the church at Corinth teach us, other people are all too happy to let us know what they think we should be doing and who they think we should be.

The capitalist myth of scarcity is an important culprit in this. Many of us have been taught that productivity is a sign of blessedness. Christians see every opportunity as a blessing from God, not to mention that we all see it as a sign that we are needed and valued by others. This tempts us to take every opportunity and request that comes our way and to assume that every opportunity is an obligation and every request is a demand.

This temptation is especially strong if our identities include marginalized and underrepresented groups. We may agree to certain roles because they are a chance for Black women and other people of color, LGBTQIA+ persons, women, disabled persons, immigrants, or poor or working-class people to have a seat at the table. We fear that if we say no, our group will not be represented.

We need to remember that while we are finite human beings, our opportunities are limitless. This means that we can say no. In fact, it means that we must say no. We can take a lesson from Paul here, too. One way to maintain appropriate boundaries is to get clear about what is actually our work. In other words, what is required, and what is desired? Whose requirement or desire is it? Why does it matter? When and how well must it be done? Are we uniquely suited to do it? Does it fit our priorities and needs at this time?

Distinguishing between what is required and what is desired not only helps us to prioritize; it also helps us to see choice and possibility where we may be tempted to see only obligation and duty. When we make choices that honor our values and commitments, we are defining ourselves and our boundaries, and we are therefore making choices that prioritize our well-being.

Today's Practice

Reflect on the following questions, using a journal or a sheet of paper. *What is your load-bearing capacity?* You can define this however makes the most sense to you—either the number of hours or the number of responsibilities you can comfortably commit to without feeling overwhelmed. *In which areas of your life or responsibilities are you overfunctioning? What are the signs that you are doing so? What might you need to release in order to operate within your limitations?*

DAY 25

Let Your No
Mean No

Let your *yes* mean yes, and your *no* mean no.
Anything more than this comes from the evil one.

MATTHEW 5:37

Boundaries exist only as long as we establish and maintain them. One way we do that is by saying no. A lot. There are people who have no problem with this. They're probably not reading this book, though. The rest of us have been socialized to constantly say yes, to be people pleasers. We feel tremendous guilt when we say no to other people, especially people we care about. Some people think that *no* is a bad word. Some parents of young children even vow to never say no to their kids because they think it is inherently negative. Guidelines on writing affirmations often tell people to avoid words such as *no* and *not* for the same reason.

But *no* is neither inherently good nor bad. As any two-year-old instinctively knows, "No!" is an important way of asserting our agency and protecting ourselves. There is no way to set, communicate, and reinforce our boundaries without saying no. It is how we tell people what we can and cannot do, accept, or allow.

I have always had a lot of difficulty saying no to others. I grew up in a family in which children were expected to do whatever authority figures said, without question. In school, saying yes opened doors for me. As a graduate student, I learned that my worth was determined by the length of my curriculum vitae, so I learned to constantly seek and accept every opportunity that was available to me. I didn't do this just for my own benefit. I prided myself on being a team player who did more than my fair share, who brought prestige to my institution, and who was doing good for the world.

But taking every invitation meant that I was overworked, resentful, and neglecting my own care. I had to learn to say no. The first step was learning to withhold my yes. When someone asked me to do something, I responded with, "That sounds good, but let me think about it and get back to you." That pause was an important safeguard against my knee-jerk tendency to say yes. It gave me time to really consider whether I had the time, energy, and interest. It also gave me time to practice my no.

These days, I have multiple ways of saying no, including the following:

- "This sounds like a great project, but the timing doesn't work."
- "My plate is full, and I can't take on any new obligations right now."
- "I'm realizing that I don't have the time to do this well. Can we reschedule?"

Increasingly, I'm able to say, "No, thank you; I won't be able to do it." I'm able to let my no just be no.

Today's Practice

What are different ways that you can say no to a future request? Identify three or four that will work for you and write them down. Repeat them aloud a few times until you memorize them (it helps to have them at the ready when you need them). If you're really feeling brave, go ahead and say no to something this week. It may even be something you've already agreed to do.

DAY 26

Protect Your Energy

At that very moment, Jesus recognized that power had
gone out from him. He turned around in the crowd and
said, "Who touched my clothes?"

MARK 5:30

Boundaries are energetic safeguards. When boundaries are rigid,
we cannot benefit from the life-giving energy of restorative relationships, and we cannot tap into our own creative potential.
When boundaries are diffuse or nonexistent, we leak energy all
over the place.

Some people are more sensitive to disruptions and imbalances
in energy than others. Jesus seems to have been one of those.
Each of the synoptic Gospels includes the story about the woman
who suffered from a bleeding disorder, who was healed simply
by touching Jesus's clothes. Every time I read the story, I am

awed by Jesus's response. Think about it: the source and wielder of all power immediately recognized that someone had taken an infinitesimal amount of his healing energy! He wanted to know who had done it and why. And when he found out, he blessed the woman. In one encounter, Jesus modeled self-awareness, assertiveness, and compassion.

Imagine if the woman had kept following Jesus around, touching him all the time, trying to draw on his power to heal every issue in her life. Undoubtedly, she would have received a different reaction from Jesus, the kind that he usually reserved for the religious elite. In that case, the woman would have been what psychiatrist Judith Orloff calls an energy vampire.[1]

Energy vampires are people who repeatedly drain us of our energy to fulfill their own needs, without contributing to our replenishment in any way. They are the people we dread spending time with because we know that they will exhaust us. And they tend to have this effect on most people. Common behaviors of energy vampires include the following:

- Often asking for help from others but rarely giving back
- Calling or texting repeatedly when in need but being unresponsive at other times
- Playing the victim in every relationship and context
- Constantly complaining that others have it better than they do while not taking responsibility for their own circumstances
- Frequently oversharing details about their lives, more than is appropriate for the relationship and situation
- Being passive-aggressive and manipulative

The term *energy vampire* is harsh but no more so than Jesus calling Peter "Satan" (Matt. 16:23) or the religious elite a "brood of vipers" (Matt. 3:7, NRSV). Indeed, like Peter—and perhaps even the religious elite—most energy vampires are not intentionally malicious. They simply do not recognize the impact that they have upon people. Setting boundaries with them is critical if we are to safeguard, manage, and direct our energy. Sometimes this means terminating the relationship. But it can also mean learning how and when to engage them in ways that mitigate their impact, clearly communicating and enforcing our boundaries and engaging in restorative self-care after time with them.

Today's Practice

Identify your energy vampires. What are the relationships and responsibilities that repeatedly drain you dry? How can you practice saying no or take action to set boundaries around them?

DAY 27

Social Media Boundaries

Everyone was raving about Jesus, so impressed were they by the gracious words flowing from his lips. They said, "This is Joseph's son, isn't it?" Then Jesus said to them, "Undoubtedly, you will quote this saying to me: 'Doctor, heal yourself. Do here in your hometown what we've heard you did in Capernaum.'" He said, "I assure you that no prophet is welcome in the prophet's hometown. . . ." When they heard this, everyone in the synagogue was filled with anger. They rose up and ran him out of town. They led him to the crest of the hill on which their town had been built so that they could throw him off the cliff. But he passed through the crowd and went on his way.

LUKE 4:22–24, 28–30

The crowd is fickle. In Luke's gospel, after forty days of fasting in the wilderness, Jesus returned to his hometown of Nazareth. On the Sabbath, he went to the synagogue as usual and began to teach. Initially, the crowd was impressed with the wisdom coming from Joseph's son. But when Jesus became more critical of the religious establishment, they turned on him and were ready to kill him. Luke does not tell us how Jesus got away. He didn't run or fight his way out. Somehow, he passed through the crowd. He walked a few towns over, to Capernaum, and continued teaching. He chose a different crowd.

We would do well to use the same practices, especially when it comes to today's technology. While there are many benefits that come with being connected through the internet and technology, social media and smartphones are innate boundary destroyers, blurring the lines between our professional and personal worlds and encouraging us to be plugged in and available to all people at all times.

Perhaps it wouldn't be so bad if it were limited to people we know. But social media platforms encourage us to reach beyond our immediate networks to form relationships with many different crowds, including people who have not established their trustworthiness: the high school classmates we weren't even friends with back in the day, the popular influencer whom we don't really like, the MAGA-loving church member, and the stranger who sent a friend request because the algorithm told them to.

Even in this digitally connected age, we have the capacity and the right to choose our own crowd. I am a firm believer in compartmentalizing social media and technology use. I keep separate professional and personal email accounts, and I refrain from checking work emails on days off (during vacations, I even delete the app). I disable smartphone notifications, and to avoid giving out my personal cell number, I use a Google Voice number, which also lets me mute notifications on my off-time.

I limit my personal Facebook page to people I know in real life. At least twice a year, I purge my friends list, culling connections that are weak, tenuous, or unclear (such as the person I met at a conference but have not had a single meaningful exchange with). I freely mute and unfollow people whose posts I don't want on my feed. That includes relatives!

My Twitter and Instagram accounts are more public facing, but they are still not free-for-alls. If I suspect that a commenter is a bot or a conservative troll looking for trouble, I block them without hesitation.

No one is entitled to our time, space, and energy, no matter how many ways Silicon Valley invents for people to access us. We get to choose our crowd.

Today's Practice

Think about your different social media and technology accounts. What purpose do you want each to serve? Who do you want to be able to contact you and when? How much time do you want to spend on social media and screens each day? Take some time to get clear about this. Then start putting your boundaries in place. Compartmentalize your social media and technology use. Make use of smartphone and social media features such as screen time limits, blocking, muting, and lists. Give yourself permission to make your networks echo chambers, especially if you are a Black woman, a person of color, LGBTQIA+, or a progressive living in conservative spaces. You have no obligation to give other people unfettered access to your life.

DAY 28

Mind Your Boundaries

You don't need us to write about loving your brothers and sisters because God has already taught you to love each other. In fact, you are doing loving deeds for all the brothers and sisters throughout Macedonia. Now we encourage you, brothers and sisters, to do so even more. Aim to live quietly, mind your own business, and earn your own living, just as I told you. That way you'll behave appropriately toward outsiders, and you won't be in need.

1 THESSALONIANS 4:9–12

Week in Review

In my favorite viral video, a man sits inside a car, his two young daughters in their car seats in the back. The youngest, August, is about two or three years old and fumbles with the buckle.

"Do you need help?" her father asks.

"No," August replies firmly. "You can help later."

Seconds pass. The dad tries again. "You want me to help?"

"No. No, thank you," she says, still struggling with the buckle.

"What do you want me to do?" the dad asks.

"Worry about yourself. I'll do this one. You drive! Worry about yourself! Go drive. Go."

People love talking about the terrible twos and the trying threes, but toddlers can teach adults some important things about boundaries. Little August was clear about what her responsibility was. She knew that she needed help with some things, but not at that moment. And when her dad repeatedly tried to cross her boundary, she let him know, clearly and firmly. As her father, he needed to make sure August was safely buckled in the car seat before they drove off, but she could also communicate her boundary about wanting to do it herself.

"Worry about yourself" is a nice way to summarize Paul's advice to the leaders of the church at Thessalonica. Other epistles exhorted fledgling congregations to tend to one another's needs, maintain unity, and hold each other accountable. The Thessalonian church, however, had no need of that. They were already doing loving deeds for one another and for the entire Macedonian area. So Paul gave them different advice: "Aim to live quietly, mind your own business, and earn your own living, just as I told you" (1 Thess. 4:11). In other words, worry about yourself.

If we do not set and maintain good boundaries, we cannot meet our own needs. And if we cannot meet our own needs, we will not behave appropriately toward others as Paul admonishes. Instead, we will become overwhelmed, resentful, and ineffective.

It is incumbent, then, upon all of us to set good boundaries, to honor our needs and limits, to say no when necessary, and to know when to ask for and receive help.

Silent Reflection

What did you learn about your boundaries in this week's reflection? In what areas of your life are you maintaining good boundary lines? In what areas are your boundaries overly rigid or diffuse? Identify one situation or relationship in which you would like to improve a boundary. What are specific ways that you can set and communicate the boundary? Write them down in a place that is accessible to you, and read them daily as a reminder.

Prayer

God, our creator and sustainer, we give you thanks for the gift of boundaries. At the dawn of creation, you brought chaos into order by establishing boundaries between the heavens and the earth; between land, sea, and sky; between day and night; between the creatures of the world; between Eve and Adam. In both dwelling among us and withdrawing from us, you have shown us that honoring our need for rest and restoration is holy and that guarding ourselves from harmful relationships and activities is divine. Enable us this day to live into this good heritage by setting our boundary lines in pleasant places. Amen.

Hymn

I SHALL NOT BE MOVED
African American Heritage Hymnal, #479

I shall not, I shall not be moved,
I shall not, I shall not be moved.
Just like a tree that's planted by the water,
I shall not be moved.
The church of God is marching, I shall not be moved.
The church of God is marching, I shall not be moved.
Just like a tree that's planted by the water,
I shall not be moved.
Come and join the army, I shall not be moved.
Come and join the army, I shall not be moved.
Just like a tree that's planted by the water,
I shall not be moved.
King Jesus is our captain, I shall not be moved.
King Jesus is our captain, I shall not be moved.

Just like a tree that's planted by the water,
I shall not be moved.
Satan had me bound, I shall not be moved.
Satan had me bound, I shall not be moved.
Just like a tree that's planted by the water,
I shall not be moved.
On my way to heaven, I shall not be moved.
On my way to heaven, I shall not be moved.
Just like a tree that's planted by the water,
I shall not be moved.

Benediction

From the beginning of time, God has rendered order out of chaos by setting boundaries. And from the very beginning, God herself has endured creation's testing of her boundaries. As you go forth into this day, may your boundary lines fall in pleasant places. And may you remember that as a cocreator with God, you have the power and authority to nudge your boundary lines when they do not. Amen.

WEEK 5

Caring for Our Emotional Selves

Over the past few weeks, we've focused on our physical health and well-being, on the internal self-care work of self-compassion, and on setting up and maintaining boundaries as a way to care for ourselves. When the demands of our lives exceed our coping capacities, we usually feel the impact first as an emotional response. We may feel overwhelmed, anxious, angry, and resentful. At the same time, we lack feelings of joy, ease, calm, peace, and contentment—the feelings that are necessary for embodying the fruits of the Spirit (Gal. 5:22–23). Wholistic self-care, then, requires us to nurture emotional wellness, which includes recognizing and learning from negative emotions and cultivating positive emotions. Our practices in this week focus on both.

DAY 29

Honoring Emotions

God! My God! It's you—
I search for you!
My whole being thirsts for you!
My body desires you
in a dry and tired land,
no water anywhere . . .
I'm fully satisfied—
as with a rich dinner.
My mouth speaks praise
with joy on my lips—

PSALM 63:1, 5

Scripture is rich with emotional language: the joy and anxiety of the psalmists, the despair and loneliness of the prophets, the peace and agony of Jesus Christ, even the sadness and vengefulness of God. While Aristotle and Saint Thomas Aquinas might have popularized the idea of God as the immovable mover, scripture does not depict God as some distant deity who puts things into action and then sits back and watches. The very idea of the incarnation is emotional. God *comes* because God *cares*, and because God comes, God *suffers* the burdens of human life.

Human beings were created in the image of God, who feels deeply. Emotions are part of our creation and serve a vital role in our survival. This is especially true of fear. The emotional experience that we label fear is the manifestation of a remarkably complex biological process that is controlled by our autonomic nervous system. When our senses perceive a threat, it triggers our brain's limbic system, setting off approximately 1,500 biochemical responses that are designed to make us temporarily faster, stronger, more alert, and more focused so that we can escape or fight the threat. That fear response is hardwired into most animals. It is why chipmunks hide at the approach of a hawk. It is also why hikers take important precautions against bears when they're on the trail. A lack of that fear can have deadly consequences.

Emotions, then, are not the enemy of reason; they are companions to it. Emotions help us to make sense of experience and to determine what to do. The same thing is true of all emotions, whether we think of them as negative or positive. Being whole, then, means having congruence between our emotions, our thoughts, our behaviors, and our bodily experiences. Therapists sometimes facilitate this by using feeling charts to help people to recognize and name their emotional experiences. It is also why we repeatedly ask, "How did that make you feel?" We're not stalling (at least not most of the time). We are trying to help people integrate head, heart, and body by connecting with and honoring their emotions.

The author of Psalm 63 illustrates this integration beautifully. The words that the psalmist uses are simultaneously emotional and physical: longing for God is experienced as thirst; praise and joy come through the lips; satisfaction is felt as a rich meal. The psalmist shows us that far from being the enemy of reasoned experience, emotions are critical to our experience of God. We need to honor them as such.

Today's Practice

Do an emotional check-in with yourself a few times today. Each time, ask yourself, "How am I feeling now?" Avoid relying on vague phrases such as *some kind of way*. Instead, identify and label your experience using specific feeling words: calm, anxious, happy, joyful, neutral, angry, frustrated, depressed, agitated, embarrassed, amused, tense, and so on. It might be helpful to google "feelings chart" to strengthen your emotional vocabulary.

DAY 30

Finding Your Joy

But the fruit of the Spirit is love, joy, peace, patience, kindness, goodness, faithfulness, gentleness, and self-control. There is no law against things like this.

GALATIANS 5:22–23

"That's incredible! Are you excited?" my White friend said. We were hanging out in our freshman dorm, and I had told her about an award I'd just received.

"Yes," I deadpanned.

She frowned. "Chanequa, why do I feel like I'm happier about this than you are?"

I didn't know what she wanted me to do. Jump up and down with glee? That was some White girl stuff. Black women didn't do that. Like Alice Walker's definition of a womanist, I was grown, responsible, in charge, serious. I was a StrongBlackWoman.

It took me a full decade after that conversation to realize that my inability to experience and display unadulterated joy was a consequence of learning to stifle my emotions and conceal vulnerability. Joy is incredibly vulnerable. It's why Michal lost all respect for David when he publicly danced before the Lord in 2 Samuel 6. In her eyes, he humiliated himself. That's what the vulnerability of joy does: it opens up the possibility that we will be humiliated and humbled. For many of us, that is terrifying. Like Michal, we think unbridled joy is hedonistic, the antithesis of authority, seriousness, discipline, and self-control.

Experiencing exuberant joy is especially difficult for those of us who struggle with self-care. Our days are so full of activity and busyness that we do not take time to revel in the bounty of our lives: the beauty of nature, the laughter of children, the warmth of sunshine, the delight of a snowflake on the tongue, the pleasure of dancing with wild abandon. Our joy is further hampered by our preoccupation with what other people think about us and our attempts to measure up to our internalized image of the ideal caregiver, the ideal leader, and the ideal disciple. We are so hard on ourselves that we assume that others are measuring us with the same stick. We're our own Michal. (Perhaps this is a good moment to remind you to check in with your self-talk and practice self-compassion.)

The writer of Galatians tries to help us reframe our relationship to joy by including it among the fruits of the Spirit. Indeed, references to joy are littered throughout the Bible. In scripture, joy is something we experience in the here and now, through our bodies, relationships, work, and celebrations. It is also something that we both remember as Christ's salvific work and anticipate as God's final redemptive act that will liberate the oppressed and restore humanity to rightful relationship with God. As a fruit of the Spirit, joy is not just a feeling; it is a discipline, something that we should seek and cultivate as an act of vulnerability and gratitude.

Today's Practice

Reflect on when you last experienced joy, not just a general sense of happiness or contentment but the type of all-encompassing, humiliation-risking joy that David embodied as he danced before God in the streets. Imagine yourself experiencing that type of joy. What would that feel like in your body? What arises for you as you imagine that type of joy? What restrains you from experiencing it? Pay attention to any messages that your inner critic gives you, and be gentle with yourself.

DAY 31

Owning Your Anger

Therefore, after you have gotten rid of lying, *Each of you must tell the truth to your neighbor* because we are parts of each other in the same body. *Be angry without sinning.* Don't let the sun set on your anger.

EPHESIANS 4:25–26

Christianity has strong African and Middle Eastern origins, but it became a powerful organized religion under the patronage of the Roman emperor Constantine I. Modern Christianity still bears the imprint of Greco-Roman culture. One example of this is dualism, the view that the world—and everything within it—can be neatly categorized into two opposing realities, for example, good and evil, spiritual and physical.

Dualism pervades much of dominant Western culture, including our view of emotions. We tend to categorize emotions as positive or negative. Positive emotions such as joy, happiness, and amusement are considered desirable, while negative emotions such as anger, embarrassment, and shame are considered undesirable. But emotions are not all good or all bad.

This is definitely true for anger. As the writer of Ephesians tells us, anger is neither sinful nor inherently bad. It is not the absence of joy, happiness, optimism, and hope. It is not the enemy of unity and fellowship. The writer is intentional about including anger as inescapable in Christian fellowship. Anger is part of truth telling, which is necessary for building up the body of Christ. The problem is not anger; it is what we do with it. "Be angry without sinning," the writer admonishes.

Anger is a normal and natural emotional reaction to a perceived threat. It is the *fight* part of the fight-flight-freeze response that God hardwired into us. Anger is a signal emotion that is trying to tell us that something is wrong (either with our situation or with ourselves) and that we need to tend to it. Often, anger is a secondary emotion, covering up more vulnerable feelings such as hurt or fear. Instead of suppressing anger, we need to own it. We should approach our anger with gentle curiosity, noticing what triggered it and how it impacts our bodies and behavior, discovering what lesson it is teaching us, and giving it what it needs to heal in that moment. We do not need to repress it or make it bigger than it is. We just need to honor it.

Joy can be a powerful companion to anger. It can set boundaries around anger, diffuse it, and direct it to an appropriate outlet. Intentionally seeking joy in the aftermath of anger can be a way of telling ourselves, "Thanks for signaling that something was wrong and that I needed protection. Now that I am safe, I am going to soothe the leftover pain by seeking out joy."

Today's Practice

Reflect upon a situation that has made you angry, preferably one that is not too recent or so volatile that it might overwhelm you. How do you know when you are angry? Where do you feel it in your body? How do you feel it emotionally? What do you normally do with your anger when it arises? How might you better honor and care for your anger?

DAY 32

Anticipate the Hard

Whatever has happened—that's what will happen again;
whatever has occurred—that's what will occur again.
There's nothing new under the sun.

ECCLESIASTES 1:9

I felt the stress and fatigue emanating from my colleague as we passed each other in the stairwell. "How are you?" I asked, even though I already knew the answer.

He sighed audibly. "Chanequa, I don't know how I'm going to make it."

I knew the feeling well. "I know. Just remember: we felt this same way last year at this time. We made it then, and we'll make it again."

At any given time, I am operating on three calendars—fiscal, academic, and liturgical—each of which has different stress points, periods when intense demands make it difficult to engage in good self-care. Academic stress, for example, peaks at the start of the semester, midterms, and finals, whereas congregational stress is often highest during Advent, Holy Week, and annual conference. Stress points are often cyclical and therefore predictable. Some are weekly, such as the evenings when we have late meetings or kids' activities. Others are more occasional: transitioning to a new job, preparing for a big presentation, organizing a big event, and so on.

As my self-care journey has evolved, I have stopped deluding myself into thinking that these points will be less stressful *this time*. I have learned to *anticipate the hard* and to accommodate it by making adjustments to my schedule, figuring out what types of supports my family and I might need during that period, and figuring out what I will need to reset afterward. Here are a few practical ways that I have learned to anticipate the hard and take some actions, which might help you in your own times of stress or busyness:

- Cook and freeze batches of muffins, soups, and stews during breaks to have available when you know you will be too busy or tired to cook.
- Make weekly meal plans and prep simple meals for the workweek, reserving time-consuming meals for your days off.
- Attend meditation retreats or put time in your calendar for reflection after—and sometimes in the midst of—high-stress periods.

- Schedule body treatments (e.g., chiropractor, massage, flotation therapy) after physically demanding travel and events.
- Maintain a relationship with a therapist for ongoing care and to facilitate quick appointments when needed.
- Keep a list of all major deadlines, to avoid having too much pile up at once.

As the writer of Ecclesiastes reminds us, whatever has happened will happen again. While that sounds somewhat defeatist, it actually can be a great help. If we pay attention to the rhythms of our lives, we learn that we can anticipate some of those seasons. And if we learn to accept our limitations and honor our needs, we may be able to weather it just a bit better.

Today's Practice

What are the hard seasons in your life—the days or periods when demands exceed your capacity and overwhelm your ability to practice self-care? It might be helpful to look at your family or organizational calendar to identify these. What supports might you need or actions might you take in order to make life a little easier during those periods?

DAY 33

Laughter Is Medicine

A joyful heart helps healing,
but a broken spirit dries up the bones.

PROVERBS 17:22

The old adage "Laughter is the best medicine" turns out to be true, at least partially. Laughter is being studied by scientists all over the world as an intervention for mental and physical health issues such as depression, anxiety, loneliness, elevated blood pressure, fatigue, sleep problems, and compromised immune function. Treatments such as laughter yoga and humor therapy are being used with a wide range of populations: cancer and dialysis patients, postpartum individuals, nursing home residents, immigrants, graduate students, even school-age children.[1]

Now, let's be clear: laughter is not a curative. It will not vanquish depression or anxiety or hypertension. But it can reduce stress hormones that are associated with multiple illnesses and poor health conditions. Laughter also increases endorphins, which relieve pain and distress. There is growing evidence that laughter—whether spontaneous or self-induced—may improve multiple aspects of our emotional and physical health.[2]

It's a good thing, then, that I have always loved to laugh. I find joy and humor in the smallest things. If I'm anywhere near small children, chances are that I'll end up laughing, because children are hilarious. I laugh in meetings when no one else does (because adults are weird, too). I definitely laugh at family gatherings because all sides of my family are full of people who are just plain fools. I even laugh when I'm nervous. That's a different type of laughter, but maybe it serves the same purpose: releasing endorphins that help soothe my nerves.

It wasn't until I was going through breast cancer treatment for the first time that I started intentionally integrating laughter into my self-care plan. During treatment, I made sure to have a good laugh at least once daily. Sometimes laughter came naturally. My husband and son are among the just plain foolish relatives, so that helped a lot. But when it didn't happen spontaneously, I sought it out, watching videos of babies or pets doing funny things. On top of the scientifically proven health benefits of laughter, giving ourselves permission to experience joy is one of the most important parts of caring for our emotional selves.

Being an introvert, I used to restrain my laughter so that it didn't draw attention. Plus, I was self-conscious about how much my gums showed when I laughed or smiled broadly. When I got serious about laughing as self-care, I let those anxieties go and started laughing with wild abandon. There are a few pictures floating around where a friend has caught me in full-throated laughter, head thrown back, eyes closed, gums just out there, getting a full dose of my daily medicine.

Today's Practice

How often do you laugh? When was the last time you did? Aim to get some laughter in your life today—seek out a funny video, watch a sitcom, listen to a comedy podcast, read a funny book, share a joke with a friend, or just enjoy a light-hearted conversation.

The Power of Play and Creativity

The LORD of heavenly forces proclaims: Old men and old women will again dwell in the plazas of Jerusalem. Each of them will have a staff in their hand because of their great age. The city will be full of boys and girls playing in its plazas.

ZECHARIAH 8:4–5

My son was ten when he stopped playing with toys. The change was gradual at first. He had already abandoned his toy kitchen and construction vehicles. But the clearest sign was when he stopped playing with his extensive train collection. By the end of his fifth grade year, we had packed his trains away and taken the rest of his toys to a consignment sale. Nowadays, the only toys in our home belong to our dog.

Humans, it seems, are the only mammals that outgrow play. During early adolescence, we become self-conscious about looking silly, childish, or—worst of all—uncool. We stop playing anything except video games, sports, and musical instruments.

I was the same as a kid. By adolescence, not only had I stopped playing; I had also stopped creating. As a kid, I had loved to draw, sew clothes for my dolls, and color. But as a high achiever, I came to believe that the only things worth doing were those I excelled at. I was, at best, average when it came to the arts. Visual-spatial skills are a challenge for me, and I cannot draw or cut a straight line to save my life. So I gave up on creativity. I told myself that I was not creative or artistic. With the exception of coloring books, I resigned myself to enjoying other people's creations rather than attempting my own.

Play and creativity, though, are vital parts of our lives and important antidotes to the impact of stress. Research indicates that play even improves our social relationships and our executive functioning, including our decision-making and emotional regulation skills.[1] The act of creation may be the most basic form of joy that exists. It is why the Judeo-Christian stories begin with creation and emphasize God's invitation to humanity to be cocreators. For those of us who tend to rely more on left-brain traits (such as logic, math and science, language and writing), seeking wholeness requires us to tap into right-brain skills, nurturing and releasing some nonliterary creative energy.

These days, I don't worry about drawing straight lines or

impressing anyone. I make jewelry, sew, paint, and craft with my Cricut. I make my own tea blends and have even started canning and preserving. I get on the floor and play with the dog until we are both worn out. My son may have given up on play, but I am learning to claim it. We might not dwell in the plazas of Jerusalem, but we can all reclaim God's promise of play.

Today's Practice

Spend some time engaging in play or doing something creative today, even if just for five minutes. Get on the floor with your kid or a pet, grab some Play-Doh or finger paint, play Frisbee or throw horseshoes, stand in front of a mirror and make silly faces, dance the zaniest you can. Don't judge your skills; just play and create!

Nurturing Emotional Wellness

So I commend enjoyment because there's nothing better for people to do under the sun but to eat, drink, and be glad. This is what will accompany them in their hard work, during the lifetime that God gives under the sun.

ECCLESIASTES 8:15

Week in Review

Many of the greatest discoveries of modern science have to do with the relationship between emotional health and physical health. We are finally learning that emotions are not simply figments or projections of our imaginations. While subjective, emotions are rooted in physiology. They are real. Moreover, our emotional health is deeply, and often inextricably, intertwined with our physical and relational health. Our physical health impacts our emotional states, our experiences and emotions can alter our physical functioning, and both of these impact our relational well-being. Wholistic self-care requires us to attend to our emotional functioning.

This can be difficult for people who have internalized the idea that emotions are antithetical to both reason and discipleship and that stoicism and self-sacrifice are the hallmarks of a good Christian. It is true that scripture cautions us against acting upon our selfish desires and doing whatever feels good without consideration of its impact upon community, as Paul warns in Galatians 5. But it is also true that the biblical witness on human emotionality is as complex as human physiology. What makes the Judeo-Christian tradition unique is its view of God's own emotionality, which ranges from hatred, anger, and vengeance to mercy, delight, and empathy. God so loved the world that God decided to enter the world alongside humanity. God's care for humanity springs from God's emotions.

Our emotions, therefore, are profoundly connected to what it means to be human and to be made in the image of God. As the writer of Ecclesiastes teaches us, life is hard and brings no small amount of suffering. Our suffering is what allows us to empathize with others, and our joy is what sustains us through suffering. Discipleship, then, requires developing awareness of and nurturing our emotional selves in ways that build us up, not just as individuals but as members of the body of Christ. Our collective peace is bound to our personal peace. So honor your emotions, all of them.

Silent Reflection

What did you notice in paying attention to your emotional experiences this week? What emotions do you find it difficult to experience and accept? What messages did you receive about these emotions when growing up, and how might you need to counter these messages? How can you be more intentional about nurturing emotional wellness? What supports might you need to care for your emotional self?

Prayer

Loving God, you have revealed yourself to us through the holy scriptures as one who feels deeply, who acts on your feelings, and who invites us to connect with you through our joy, our sadness, our anxiety, even our anger. Help us to properly steward the gift of emotions—to be angry without sinning, to nurture joy and peace, to delight in play and creativity, and to care for all of creation in the way that you care for us. Amen.

•••

Hymn

JOYFUL, JOYFUL, WE ADORE YOU
African American Heritage Hymnal, #120

Joyful, joyful, we adore You,
God of glory, Lord of love;
Hearts unfold like flow'rs before You,
Op'ning to the sun above.
Melt the clouds of sin and sadness;
Drive the dark of doubt away;
Giver of immortal gladness,
Fill us with the light of day!
All Your works with joy surround You,
Earth and heav'n reflect Your rays,
Stars and angels sing around You,
Center of unbroken praise;
Field and forest, vale and mountain,
Flow'ry meadow, flashing sea,
Chanting bird and flowing fountain,
Praising You eternally.
Always giving and forgiving,
Ever blessing, ever blest,
Wellspring of the joy of living,
Ocean depth of happy rest!
Loving Father, Christ our Brother,
Let Your light upon us shine;
Teach us how to love each other,
Lift us to the joy divine.

Mortals join the mighty chorus,
Which the morning stars began;
God's own love is reigning o'er us,
Joining people hand in hand.
Ever singing, march we onward
Victors in the midst of strife;
Joyful music leads us sunward
In the triumph song of life.

Benediction

You have been reminded that you were created in the image of the God who feels deeply and who has created humanity with the capacity for deep emotion. May God bless you with the wisdom to join your emotion with your reason, with compassion for yourself as you go through the ups and downs of life, and with joy, love, peace, kindness, goodness, faithfulness, gentleness, and self-control. Amen.

WEEK 6

Caring for Our Minds

As Christians, we are often told that our minds cannot be trusted, that they are the enemy of our hearts and the enemy of faith. But our minds are an important part of who we are. The complexity of our minds is what separates us from the rest of creation. It is also, unfortunately, what tempts us to think that we are exempt from the need for care. When we are busy to the point of self-neglect, our minds are often full, racing with thoughts of what we need to do. Experiencing the peace promised to us by Christ requires having calm minds. This week, we will explore mindfulness practices as strategies for cultivating mental habits of stillness, silence, presence, thoughtfulness, and loving-kindness.

DAY 36

Stillness Is the Better Part

She had a sister named Mary, who sat at the Lord's feet and listened to his message. By contrast, Martha was preoccupied with getting everything ready for their meal. So Martha came to him and said, "Lord, don't you care that my sister has left me to prepare the table all by myself? Tell her to help me." The Lord answered, "Martha, Martha, you are worried and distracted by many things. One thing is necessary. Mary has chosen the better part. It won't be taken away from her."

LUKE 10:39–42

Modern life moves at a frenetic pace. For many Americans, our days are filled with activity from the time we awake until we go to bed. We are constantly on the go and always in a rush. Even before the dawn of the gig economy and hustle culture, our schedules were overbooked and our kids were overprogrammed. Now, it's worse. We think being our best selves means maximizing productivity by filling every possible moment with some purposeful activity. We can't enjoy hobbies without feeling pressured to turn them into side hustles. And then 2020 came, and with it a global pandemic, which ground many things in our lives to a halt. For many people, the extra time was at first a blessing, bringing us freedom from commutes, meetings, and other obligations. But we quickly filled that freedom with videoconferences and projects like baking the perfect sourdough loaf or writing the great American novel.

Many of us are uncomfortable with silence and stillness, so we live with constant stimulation. When we are alone, we turn on music or television to keep us company. When we are in the same room with others, we feel compelled to fill the space with chatter at all times. Introverts are not immune from this; we just fill the silence with internal chatter or by distracting ourselves with other activity.

Avoiding silence and stillness is a way of running from ourselves and our realities, but self-care is impossible without self-awareness. Self-awareness includes awareness of what is happening in our minds, with our bodies, and in our relationships. Self-awareness helps us to become aware of our internal scripts (such as those that tell us our worth is dependent on our productivity), our bodily sensations and needs, our emotions, and our reactions to the external world.

We can easily fool ourselves into thinking that chronic busyness is okay if it benefits others. That is especially the case for Christians who struggle with self-care: we are busy on others' behalf. We are caring for loved ones, serving in our churches and communities, advocating for justice, and doing our part (and more) at work. We are often doing the very type of service that Jesus bid us to do.

So was Martha. When Jesus visited her home, Martha wanted to show him the type of hospitality that he had told his disciples to expect just a few verses earlier in Luke 10. Martha was doing good things! Unfortunately, she was doing so many good things that she was anxious, resentful of her sister, and distracted from what matters most: time with Jesus. She needed to be still in order to love God, to love her sister, and to love herself. So do we.

Today's Practice

Spend some time practicing silence and stillness today. Take five minutes to sit in silence, without looking at your phone, tablet, or television. No reading or radio, either. Just notice what it feels like to be in stillness and silence. If sitting in silence is too difficult, consider doing an activity in complete silence, perhaps washing the dishes, preparing dinner, walking, driving to work, or even eating a meal. During that time, direct your focus toward the task at hand and notice what arises for you.

DAY 37

Mindfulness Matters

More than anything you guard, protect your mind,
for life flows from it.

PROVERBS 4:23

A truly sustainable self-care practice requires us to know and respond to our needs. That is easier said than done for people who have been socialized to focus more on others than on themselves. When I began my self-care journey at the age of thirty, I quickly realized that I did not know my own needs or desires. Instead, I made decisions on the basis of what I knew about other people's needs and desires. For example, when going out to eat with my husband, I chose the chair that I knew he would not want to sit in. When I set meeting times, I always started by asking the other person what worked best for them. Two decades later, I am more in touch with my needs but also still learning myself. In many ways, the self-care journey is a lifelong experience of learning and relearning what our needs are as we go through different stages and situations. Self-care is a journey of self-awareness.

Mindfulness practices such as sitting meditation, body scans, journaling, and mindful movement are powerful tools for cultivating self-awareness. Jon Kabat-Zinn, the founder of mindfulness-based stress reduction, defines mindfulness as "the awareness that emerges through paying attention on purpose, in the present moment, and nonjudgmentally to the unfolding of experience moment by moment."[1] Mindfulness-based practices have extensive health benefits, including reductions in blood pressure, heart rate, blood cortisol (the stress hormone), anxiety, depression, and chronic pain. They also help to increase compassion and cognitive flexibility, which Christians should recognize as cousins of the fruits of the Spirit.

Another way to understand mindfulness is to think about its antithesis: mindlessness. Have you had the experience of driving somewhere but once you arrived at your destination, you couldn't remember how you got there? We can spend a lot of life like that, on autopilot, lost in the reverie of thoughts and emotions, distracted from the present by our multitasking and excessive responsibility. Mindfulness is the antidote to autopilot. It is a way of fulfilling the wisdom of Proverbs 4:23: "More than anything you guard, protect your mind, for life flows from it."

Mindfulness is also the anchor that keeps us grounded in the present moment. It helps us notice, name, and accept the experience of the present moment. It gives us practice in releasing our need for control and freeing ourselves from self-judgment. Mindfulness does not mean controlling or stopping our thoughts but rather learning to notice them without judgment.

Today's Practice

Make a commitment to practice at least five minutes of sitting meditation today. A good guided meditation to start with is the breath awareness practice in the self-care resource guide on my website, www.drchanequa.com. If sitting in stillness is too difficult for you, instead you can try five minutes of the walking meditation practice available in the resource guide.

DAY 38

Minding the Body

No one ever hates his own body, but feeds it and takes care of it just like Christ does for the church because we are parts of his body.

EPHESIANS 5:29-30

"When did the problem start?" I hate it when doctors ask that question. I rarely notice when a symptom begins or how it develops. It is only when pain or discomfort is practically yelling at me that I pay attention.

For much of my life, I have been disconnected from my body. I live in my head, in the world of ideas and words, something that has served me well academically. As a student, I knew how to buckle down and ignore my physiological needs and desires in order to get my work done. I excelled at minimizing anything that might interfere with study time or jeopardize my academic goals, including sleep, rest, exercise, touch, and sex. The only physical need I attended to was eating. That one I could do while studying.

The messages that I received from my church, family, and culture did not help. Like many Christian girls, I internalized the idea that my body was something shameful. On top of that, I was a Black girl with kinky hair and big hips before the natural hair movement and the BBL (Brazilian butt lift) craze made either of those attractive. As I briefly mentioned earlier, starting in my teens, I put a lot of focus on hiding my body—trying to tame the kinks with damaging relaxers and curling irons, covering my hips with long, loose clothing, and wearing only neutral-toned makeup.

Many of us have been socialized away from our bodies, taught instead to focus upon the needs of other bodies and to take pride in caring more for other people and institutions than we do for ourselves. It is self-neglect, but we call it responsibility, discipline, drive, even discipleship. Scripture, though, does not teach us to hate our bodies. Even Paul, the champion of self-denial, says that we should feed and take care of our bodies with the love of Christ!

As a two-time breast cancer survivor, I have learned that I cannot afford to ignore my body. But paying attention to my body is not something that comes naturally. It is a skill that I have to develop and hone. Body scan practices have helped me to do that. A body scan is a guided mindfulness practice in which we systematically pay attention to what is happening with each part of our bodies. For the first fifteen years of my meditation practice, I avoided doing body scans because of the time involved (twenty to forty-five minutes). A few years ago, though, I began practicing it once per week. Soon, I felt more connected to my body, more aware of what I was feeling and what I needed, and better able to respond to the question that doctors love to ask, "When did the problem start?"

Today's Practice

Do a body scan meditation. You can find one in the self-care resource guide on my website, www.drchanequa.com. You will need to find a comfortable place where you can lie down or sit in a relaxed position. The practice may be difficult at first, but challenge yourself to make it through at least a ten-minute practice, and then gradually work up to longer meditations.

DAY 39

Loved and Loving

He has told you, human one, what is good and
what the LORD requires from you:
to do justice, embrace faithful love, and walk humbly
   with your God.

MICAH 6:8

As I previously mentioned, one of the unexpected benefits of
my self-care journey was that it made me more caring toward
others. When we care for ourselves as an act of gratitude to
the loving God who created us in their own image, we become
more compassionate toward ourselves and others.

A concept related to compassion is loving-kindness. Loving-
kindness (or *metta* in Pali) meditation is a traditional practice
in Buddhism, possibly as old as mindfulness of breathing. But
the concept of loving-kindness is also strongly Judeo-Christian.

The *HarperCollins Bible Dictionary* defines loving-kindness as devotion, loyalty, and covenantal faithfulness. The Hebrew word for it, *khesed*, appears in the Hebrew canon (i.e., the Christian Old Testament) over 200 times. *Khesed* is translated as loving-kindness 30 times in the King James Version of the Bible. Most frequently, it is translated as mercy (145 times) or simply as kindness (38 times). In almost every case, it is used to describe a characteristic of God. In Micah 6, though, humans are enjoined to emulate God's loving-kindness. Of course, in the New Testament, both love and kindness are listed among the fruits of the Spirit. Clearly, loving-kindness is a characteristic that Christians ought to embody.

Mindfulness offers us a set of practices for developing loving-kindness. Loving-kindness meditation consists of repeating a set of statements to oneself, such as these:

May you be happy.
May you be healthy.
May you be safe and free from harm.
May you be at peace.

These statements are not just affirmations, which are mantras we repeat to ourselves with a goal of changing our behavior. In loving-kindness meditation, we direct these phrases toward various groups: ourselves, beings whom we find it easy to love (i.e., our friends, family members, partners), beings with whom we have difficulty (i.e., our enemies), and all of creation. We repeat the phrases on behalf of ourselves and others, with no expectation that we can change either. As Christians in particular, we offer them up to God as prayers of blessing for ourselves, for others, and for the world. We ask the God of all to grant us—and all of creation—happiness, health, safety, and peace. The more we ask, the more we desire it for ourselves and others, the more loving we become.

Today's Practice

Practice a loving-kindness meditation. You can find one in the mindfulness resources in the self-care resource guide on my website, www.drchanequa.com. As you become familiar with the practice, you can do it on your own using the phrases suggested earlier.

DAY 40

Wise Speech

With lots of words comes wrongdoing,
but the wise restrain their lips.

PROVERBS 10:19

As part of my deepening mindfulness practice, I participate in a silent retreat each year. If being silent among a group of strangers for three to six days sounds terrifying, you're not alone. It took ten years of practicing meditation before I stopped procrastinating and did a silent retreat. Being on retreat is both agony and ecstasy, especially in the first few days as you settle into silence. By the end, though, I have difficulty emerging from the quiet and calm. Retreats fill me with deep feelings of peace, clarity, and alertness. It is hard to reenter the busy world after that.

During the height of the COVID-19 pandemic, many retreat

centers shifted their offerings online. I thought it was hard being in a retreat center, but practicing silence at home was an entirely different level of hard, especially when my middle schooler was in the next room doing remote classes and my dog could not figure out why I was not speaking to her.

There were times when it was impossible not to speak. In these instances, the instruction was to practice right—or wise—speech. According to Pamela Ayo Yetunde and Cheryl Giles, editors of the groundbreaking book *Black and Buddhist*, right speech includes both refraining from speech that is harmful to ourselves and others and speaking in ways that are truthful, beneficial, and compassionate.[1] Practicing wise speech means that we abstain from lying, deception, idle chatter, and gossip. It is not about being nice for the sake of niceness; it acknowledges and allows for anger but refrains from abusive and mean-hearted rhetoric. Wise speech aims at being constructive, not destructive.

During these at-home retreats, combining silence with wise speech made me slow down. I had to think about what was helpful and necessary to say before speaking. I had to anticipate the impact of my words upon those who were present to hear them. When I finally spoke, I had to discipline myself to say no more than was necessary.

The commitment to wise speech helped me to be more aware of myself and the people in my environment. I learned to listen to others fully before formulating my own thoughts. Allowing space for silence disrupted my normal tendency to abruptly shift topics, go off on tangents, and backtrack while speaking. The effect persisted for a few days after retreat. As I moved back into my regular activities, I felt clearer and calmer in my interactions with others. I understood other people better because I truly listened to what they were saying, and other people understood me better because my speech was thoughtful.

Scripture repeatedly admonishes us to exercise wisdom and restraint in speech. Mindfulness is the tool we can use to live into that command.

Today's Practice

Spend part of the day in silence, even if it is just an hour. Refrain from talking, emailing, texting, and even being on social media during your period of silence. Tell others around you what you will be doing so that they will be prepared for and supportive of your practice. When speaking is necessary, practice wise speech.

DAY 41

Meditating on the Word

Oh, how I love your law!

It is my meditation all day long.

Your commandment makes me wiser than my enemies,

For it is always with me.

PSALM 119:97–98 (NRSV)

Every mindfulness practice uses an *anchor* to keep us grounded in the present: the breath in breath awareness meditation, the body in body scans, the sensation of movement in yoga and walking meditation. We can use the Word as our anchor, too! The Christian tradition has several contemplative practices that use words of our faith as anchors, including centering prayer, breath prayer, and lectio divina.

Centering prayer is a receptive form of prayer that pairs silence with a sacred word. The sacred word can be any word connected with our faith, for example, *God*, *Jesus*, *Holy Spirit*, *faith*, *love*, *joy*, *peace*. It can be chosen deliberately, or we can let it arise at the Spirit's prompting after prayer. As with sitting meditation, we sit in silence, drawing our attention toward God by repeating our chosen word. At the same time, we remain aware of what is happening within us. When we find ourselves drifting off into thought, we return to our sacred word.

Breath prayer can be done as a sitting practice or while engaged in any rhythmic, repetitive activity (such as walking, washing dishes, or folding laundry). With breath prayer, we repeat a short phrase (four or five words) in tune with our in-breath and out-breath. Phrases from scriptures and hymns make great breath prayers. For example, we might say, "Come, Holy Spirit," or "Amazing grace, how sweet the sound."

With lectio divina, the anchor is a short passage of scripture, possibly from the lectionary readings, a book of the Bible that we are reading through, or any passage that feels like it has some timely wisdom. There are four phases in lectio divina. In the first phase, *lectio*, we read the text slowly, savoring each word, making mental note of any words or images that catch our attention. In the second phase, *meditatio*, we read the passage again and then silently reflect on what God may be saying to us through the passage. In the third phase, *oratio*, we reread the passage and then respond to it verbally, perhaps through journaling our reflections or praying. In the final phase, *contemplatio*, we read the passage again and then sit in silent contemplation for several minutes.

Meditating on the Word is particularly powerful when it is combined with regular silent meditation practice. Mindfulness helps us to be in stillness and silence and to develop moment-by-moment awareness of our internal and external experience. Meditating on the Word ushers us into divine presence in a slightly different way. It slows us down so that we can hear what God is saying to us through God's Word. It reminds us that God is still speaking to us through the holy scriptures.

Today's Practice

Spend some time meditating on the Word today, using one of the techniques just described. You can find several recorded practices in the mindfulness section of the self-care resource guide on my website, www.drchanequa.com.

DAY 42

The Skilled Mind

Those with insight find prosperity;
those who trust the LORD are blessed.
The skilled mind is called discerning,
And pleasant speech enhances teaching.

PROVERBS 16:20–21

Week in Review

I was eight years old when I learned that the world was not safe. It was 1980, and someone was killing Black children in Atlanta.[1] Many of the murders happened in the East Atlanta area, where both sets of my grandparents lived and only a few minutes from my house in Decatur. The Atlanta child murders changed life for an entire generation of Black children. We were no longer allowed to go outside unsupervised. Forty years later, each time

I walk outside, I have to confront my fears. And boy, do they show up! Every noise, every shadow, every rustle of a tree is a reason to fear, a possible threat lurking in a suburban yard. Figments of an imagination scarred by trauma, my response to a world I do not feel safe in.[2]

There was a time when, though unaware of my fear, I acted on it nonetheless. I would refuse to walk, often using other excuses or rationalizations. "It's too hot." "It's too cold." "I'm too busy." Or, even worse, my unmetabolized anxiety would leak over into other areas of my life, closing me off to experience or prompting me to lash out in frustration and irritability. Nowadays, I notice my fear, acknowledge my body's response. I breathe into it. I take note of my surroundings and remind myself that here, now, I am safe. I keep walking.

Mindfulness is not idle. It takes a lot of work to be present and to notice what is happening in our minds, in our bodies, in our interactions, and in our surroundings. It takes strength to be willing to see things as they are and to sit with the discomfort rather than run away from it. It takes discipline to refrain from acting or speaking on our every impulse.

Many of us have been conditioned to view our minds as the enemy of Christian discipleship. We are told that we think too much and we ask too many questions. But Jesus himself instructs us to love God with our mind. *"And you must love the Lord your God with all your heart, with all your being, with all your mind, and with all your strength"* (Mark 12:30). Loving God, loving our neighbor, and loving ourselves requires a skilled mind and wise speech. Mindfulness helps us to develop both.

Silent Reflection

What have you noticed in your practice of mindfulness this week? Where did you experience difficulty in doing these practices? What types of thoughts, feelings, and sensations arose during practice? Were there any patterns? Which practices were especially helpful to you, and how might you integrate them into your life?

Prayer

God of wisdom, out of all your creation it is humans whom you have gifted with complexity of thought and speech. We confess before you today that we do not always use this gift well. Help us to overcome mindlessness and to nurture skillfulness of mind and speech. Teach us to be still, to connect with the wisdom you have planted within us, to discern the ways that you continue to speak to us, and to embody kindness, gentleness, and self-control in our interactions with others. Amen.

Hymn

BLESSED QUIETNESS
African American Heritage Hymnal, #374

Refrain:
Blessed quietness,
Holy quietness,
What assurance in my soul;
On the stormy sea,
Jesus speaks to me,
And the billows cease to roll.
Joys are flowing like a river,
Since the Comforter has come;
He abides with us forever,
Makes the trusting heart His home.
Bringing life and health and gladness
All around this heav'nly Guest
Conquered unbelief and sadness
Changed our weariness to rest.
Like the rain that falls from heaven,
Like the sunlight from the sky,
So the Holy Spirit's given
Coming on us from on high.
See, a fruitful field is growing,
Blessed fruit of righteousness;
And the streams of life are flowing
In the lonely wilderness
What a wonderful salvation,

When we always see His face,
What a perfect habitation,
What a quiet resting place.

Benediction

There is no greater command than this: that we love the Lord our God with all our heart, all our mind, all our soul, and all our strength. As you go forth in obedience to this command, may you develop and nurture the skilled discernment of a wise mind and the peace of a quiet spirit. Amen.

WEEK 7

Practicing
Self-Care for
Everyday Life

Self-care is not a special occasion. It is a way of life. Or, at least, it should be. The way that we have approached self-care in this book—as an act of sacred, subversive stewardship that is rooted in our creation in the divine image—is countercultural. That means that we are unlikely to find supports for self-care built into our lives. If anything, modern living is designed to undermine our health and well-being at nearly every turn. Practicing consistent self-care requires intentionality. In this final week, then, we will turn our attention to strategies that will help us to sustain self-care for the long haul.

DAY 43

Making Time
for Self-Care

Where your treasure is, there your heart will be also.

MATTHEW 6:21

For several years, my family ate takeout at least three days per week. It was rarely intentional; our goal was to cook healthy meals at home whenever possible. We would start well, going to the market on the weekends and stocking up on produce and proteins to last the week. By midweek, though, we would be too tired and time-pressed to do anything other than peruse menus and place an order for the fat- and sugar-filled comfort foods that our stress hormones were demanding. Eventually, we would discard the vegetables that had rotted in the fridge and then repeat the cycle. There's no shame in taking a break from cooking or ordering comfort food from time to time, but we were getting into an unhealthy habit that we needed to address.

One day I had an epiphany: the reason that I could not maintain healthy eating patterns was that I had not prioritized it. If I truly valued healthy eating, I would make time for it the same way that I did other high-priority tasks. I would put it on the schedule and protect the time that was dedicated to it. Since I am a self-avowed planner junkie, I put my obsession to work for me. I modified my weekly schedule template—a one-page chart that depicts my ideal version of how I will structure my time during each workday—to include time for grocery shopping, meal preparation, and eating.

Self-care takes time. Whether it is eating, exercise, sleep, prayer, relationships, medical appointments—it all takes time. Our challenge is to align our time with our self-care priorities. We have to figure out what our treasure is, because there our hearts will be also.

My schedule template is a visible reminder of what I claim to treasure. It includes my work responsibilities but also my self-care commitments: meditation, exercise, sleep, eating healthy meals with my family, healthcare appointments. Sticking to the schedule is a way of setting boundaries around my time and my priorities, but I do not adhere to it rigidly. I have to be flexible, allowing myself to deviate from the schedule so that I can adapt to the demands of life, as well as the spontaneous delights that arise. Having the schedule, though, helps me to anticipate how my rhythms will be impacted when life disrupts my routine. For example, I avoid early morning meetings because they necessitate skipping my devotional and stretching routine. On the occasions that I have to deviate from the schedule, the template provides a point of return. I practice. I deviate. I return to practice.

Like our bodies, time is God's gift to us. Last week, we started the work of separating our productivity from our worth, and now, giving ourselves permission to use that time for our own care and nurture is an act of gratitude to God for both time and our bodies.

Today's Practice

How does your time align with your values? How might you put self-care on your schedule today? Identify either a onetime or regular practice, and make room for it in your schedule. If you keep a planner (paper or electronic), write it in.

DAY 44

Automating Self-Care

If an ax is dull and one doesn't sharpen it first, then one must exert more force. It's profitable to be skillful and wise.

ECCLESIASTES 10:10

I am a planner, which means I exert a lot of energy trying to anticipate what comes next, making decisions, and then making contingency plans for my decisions. My brain is like one big Tetris game, constantly strategizing how to fit the different pieces of my life together to prevent chaos. Taking on this role in my family means that effort is multiplied, which can be rewarding in its own way but stressful.

Even if you don't consider yourself a planner, decisions about self-care can be daunting, especially when you're exhausted or overwhelmed by stress. Take eating, for example. You have to plan each meal, every day of your life. You have to inventory your pantry and refrigerator, make grocery lists, decide where and when to shop, and then do the shopping. If you share meals with other people, you have to negotiate different dietary requirements and preferences. Yes, these are privileged problems, but they are problems nonetheless. Each decision point adds a layer of complexity—and stress—to a simple task.

One way to cut through the decision-making stress is to follow Kendra Adachi's suggestion of *deciding once* from her book *The Lazy Genius Way.* Deciding once is a way of automating our self-care and removing some of the stress and time involved in making decisions about it. For example, we can lay out our clothes for the week, set up our morning coffee the night before work, schedule a weekly appointment with a trainer, or establish a dedicated space and time for meditation and prayer.

My family adopted this strategy for meal planning, and it was a game changer. Rather than come up with a completely different meal plan every day, we decided once on a pattern that we repeat weekly: time-intensive meals on Sundays, pasta on Mondays, Tex-Mex on Tuesdays, and so on. All we do each week is figure out which variations of those meals to make. We even include a planned takeout day.

Sustaining self-care requires both skill and wisdom. As scripture reminds us, if we are working with a dull axe, we have to put in more work to get the job done. When it comes to self-care, deciding once can be the sharpening that makes it easier.

Today's Practice

Identify one area where you can automate or shortcut your decision-making. If it is something that you are already doing, celebrate that as a self-care win!

DAY 45

Maintaining Margin

The plans of the diligent end up in profit,
but those who hurry end up with loss.

PROVERBS 21:5

If you go to a bookstore looking for books on time management, you will likely end up in the business section of the store. Capitalism views time as a commodity that can be spent, wasted, maximized, and managed. Consequently, most time management approaches focus upon maximizing productivity and efficiency, upon doing more in less time.

When I was a doctoral student, I had to balance full-time classes with clinical practicum, research, a part-time job, church membership, and, eventually, marriage. I had too much to do and very little time to do it, so I became a master at multitasking (or so I thought). I took my statistics textbooks to my part-time job as a substance abuse counselor, my wedding planner binder to conferences, and my dissertation *everywhere*. Every moment had to be filled; it was the only way to get it all done.

When I began my self-care journey, it was with that multi-tasking mentality. I took a strategy from one of those time management books and filled every waking moment with some planned activity. Self-care became another task to force into an already crowded agenda. I had learned to align my time with my priorities, but I had too many priorities. The result was that even with plenty of self-care practices, I was stressed, fatigued, and harried.

I needed margin. Margin is free space, time that is intentionally left open to allow us to slow down, to breathe, and to recenter throughout our day. Margin allows us to nurture relationships with friends, family, and coworkers rather than speed past them on the way to the next thing. Margin leaves room for the unexpected, the crises and emergencies that have a habit of showing up when our schedules are tight, or even for the unexpected joys.

Maintaining margin is a discipline of restraint that does not come easily to overachievers who struggle with self-care. We have to restrain our impulse to say yes to everything and to fill every available space with obligation. We have to restrain our internal pressure to be all things to all people. It's setting a boundary around our time. We have to block off chunks of time, to say no more than we say yes, and to commit to significantly less than we think we are capable of doing.

We cannot create time, but with diligence, we can create margin. And margin is where the real profit is.

Today's Practice

Find a way to create some margin in your schedule today. Here are a few ideas for how you can do this:

- Give yourself extra time for your commute so that you are not rushed.
- End a meeting or activity ten to fifteen minutes before your next commitment to allow for transition time.
- Take your lunch break away from your desk or work area.
- Add one or two fifteen-minute breaks to your workday during which you pause work and move around.
- Put less on your to-do list than you think you can accomplish in a day or week.
- Use a pomodoro timer app to set cycles of work and break time. The pomodoro technique breaks work into short intervals (often twenty-five minutes) separated by brief breaks (often five minutes).
- Cancel, reschedule, or delegate a task or meeting that is not high priority.
- Un-volunteer for something that you have committed to do. Be sure to exercise compassion toward yourself and toward others. Try to do this in a way that does not leave people in the lurch.

DAY 46

The Power
to Cease

So you see that a sabbath rest is left open for God's
people. The one who entered God's rest also rested from
his works, just as God rested from his own. Therefore,
let's make every effort to enter that rest so that no one
will fall by following the same example of disobedience.

HEBREWS 4:9–11

During my first year in seminary, I was forced to go on a silent
retreat. As I mentioned earlier, I've grown to love the idea of retreat and being in silence. But back then, the timing was wrong.
I had a ton of work to do and needed my weekend to do it. I tried
explaining that to the seminary chaplain, but she wasn't trying
to hear it. So I showed up, simmering with resentment (as many

of my classmates were!). Then, in our opening worship session, just before we settled into silence, the chaplain looked at us and said: "Sabbath is a commandment right along with 'Thou shalt not kill' and 'Thou shalt not steal.' But you don't plan to ignore those today, do you?" It was a Damascus moment for me.

Genesis teaches us that God deliberately instituted the Sabbath as a day of rest, not just for creation but for God's own self. God rested. Christ rested. Modern Christianity, though, has largely excised the Sabbath from our spiritual practices. Consequently, many of us have not developed the discipline of ceasing, which is vital to healthy self-care.

In *Keeping the Sabbath Wholly*, Marva Dawn identifies four aspects of Sabbath observance: ceasing, resting, embracing, and feasting. At its core, Sabbath is about ceasing from labor. It is also, as Dawn points out, about ceasing from striving, from anxiety and worry, and from the pressure to be productive. Sabbath is an invitation to cease our activity, to rest in God's peaceful presence, to embrace a countercultural way of living, and to feast on the beauty and joy of God's world and the eschatological hope of God's kin-dom.

Sustaining self-care requires ceasing. It is not that we lack self-care because we are lazy, neglectful, or irresponsible with our time. We lack self-care because we do not know how to cease. We do not know how to cease work, how to cease the pressures of productivity and consumption, how to cease self-criticism and self-judgment, how to cease saying yes, how to cease the belief that we are not good enough.

We have the power to cease. God has gifted us with this power and invited us . . . no, commanded us to use it. Let us all make every effort to exercise that power so that we will not be disobedient.

Today's Practice

Find a way to practice ceasing today. Here are a few ideas for this practice:

- Pause during the day for a mindfulness practice such as centering prayer or breath awareness meditation.
- Take an actual lunch break.
- If you have a flexible work schedule or are prone to working long hours, set a time when you will end work for the day, and stick to it. If it is your day off, refrain from work.
- Refrain from compulsively checking your smartphone, email, or social media accounts. If you need to do any of these for work, set predetermined times for doing so and refrain at all other times.
- Pay attention to your self-talk. Notice when you are overthinking, being critical of yourself or others, or worrying. Try to interrupt these thoughts (even if for only a few minutes) by breathing deeply and repeating an affirmation such as *I am grounded in the present moment.*

DAY 47

Care in Community

Many people were coming and going, so there was no time to eat. He said to the apostles, "Come by yourselves to a secluded place and rest for a while." They departed in a boat by themselves for a deserted place. Many people saw them leaving and recognized them, so they ran ahead from all the cities and arrived before them. When Jesus arrived and saw a large crowd, he had compassion on them because they were like sheep without a shepherd. Then he began to teach them many things.

MARK 6:31–34

Self-care is difficult because we do not live in a world that supports it. Reclaiming the right to self-care often feels like a battlefield, where we play defense against other people's expectations and demands. In a society where nearly everyone is care deprived, people do not easily respect, honor, or support our attempts to care for ourselves. This becomes painfully obvious when we try to say no to some people. They respond with resentment, anger, accusation, and encroachments upon our boundaries. This is why the *self* part of self-care is so important. When it comes to self-care, it is like Gee Money says in the 1990s film *New Jack City*: "We all we got!"

Ceasing is hard when intrusions are relentless. Jesus and his disciples learned that. In Mark 6, upon realizing that serving the crowd had given them no time to eat, Jesus instructed his disciples to retreat for a while. But the crowd anticipated Jesus's destination and ran to meet him there! Think about that: they intentionally decided to pursue Jesus so that they could get more from him.

Of course, Jesus had empathy for the people's needs, so he and the disciples kept ministering. No one ate, and eventually, everyone was hungry. In trying to serve the people, Jesus and the disciples had set aside their own needs. At the same time, in trying to get their needs for healing and deliverance met, the crowd had ignored the need to nourish their bodies. They were not being inconsiderate or selfish. It probably did not occur to them that Jesus and the disciples needed rest and nourishment, because they were oblivious to their own needs for the same.

There was only one solution: they had to do it together. Jesus and the disciples pulled out their dinner, told everyone to sit down, and tended their bodies as a community.

When our self-care efforts face resistance from other people, it is often because those people need to learn to care for themselves. We can be a blessing to them by encouraging them to practice self-care, perhaps even along with us. This is the beauty of sacred self-care: it is communal. When we experience its benefit, our love for God's people compels us to want others to experience it as well. Self-love becomes neighbor love, drawing us closer to one another and closer to Christ.

Today's Practice

Become an ambassador for sacred self-care. If you live with other people, consider ways that you can collectively support each other's health and well-being. This might mean each person taking responsibility for cooking dinner once or twice per week. Don't exclude the kids; teenagers can cook simple meals (even if it means you are eating spaghetti every week), and young kids can help with meal planning and prep.

You can also become an ambassador for self-care at work, at church, and in other settings. Pay attention to how workloads and meeting schedules impact the health of the community, and encourage the adoption of healthier patterns. This could be as simple as speaking up when a committee or team suggests working through lunch. At church, you might encourage the congregation to refrain from holding committee meetings on Sundays or, even better, to choose one day of the week when no meetings or events will be scheduled.

You might also practice communal care by finding accountability partners. Even if it is just one person, find someone who also wants to improve their self-care. You can start by reading this book together. Check in with each other weekly to discuss your self-care goals and your progress. Celebrate your improvements!

DAY 48

The Self-Care
Rule of Life

Then the LORD answered me and said,
Write a vision, and make it plain upon a tablet
so that a runner can read it.
There is still a vision for the appointed time;
it testifies to the end;
it does not deceive.
If it delays, wait for it;
for it is surely coming; it will not be late.

HABAKKUK 2:2–3

I spent the first dozen years of my self-care journey learning what
I need. Eventually, I identified a collection of practices and habits,
but there was no rhythm or organization to them. Consequently,
there were frequent failures and lapses in my self-care. I needed a

strategy for maintaining consistency. It turned out that the very thing I needed had a long history in Christianity: a rule of life.

Since at least the fifth century, various leaders of monastic communities have developed a *rule* that governed and organized the life of their members. By the ninth century, the Rule of Saint Benedict governed monastic communities across Europe. Each rule set expectations and guidelines on how the monks were to cultivate their relationships with God, to live in harmony with one another, and to serve the world. They included instruction on spiritual practices that monks should observe (e.g., prayer, meditation, fasting) as well as the virtues that they were to cultivate (e.g., humility, simplicity, charity).

At some point, people realized that it was not only monks who benefited from living by a rule of life. In *Soul Feast*, Marjorie Thompson points out that leaders such as Dorothy Day and Martin Luther King Jr. developed rules meant to sustain lives of faithful activism and ministry. By the end of the twentieth century, the revival of spiritual formation among Protestants led many Christians to adapt rules for personal use.

Because the primary aim of a rule of life is to promote growth in holiness, they usually emphasize spiritual disciplines. As we have learned, though, humans are not just spiritual beings. We are body-mind-spirits who live in a web of relationships with our families, our communities, and the broader world. Thus, a rule of life should support holiness *and* wholeness. A Self-Care Rule of Life, then, is a pattern of activities, habits, disciplines, and practices that promote spiritual, physical, emotional, mental, and relational wholeness. And while the risk of any "rule" is that it can become a rigid, legalistic mandate, a Self-Care Rule of

Life should instill a sense of freedom and well-being rather than obligation and stress.

My personal Self-Care Rule of Life keeps me accountable to the practices necessary for my wholeness and my vitality for ministry. Some practices are daily (such as staying hydrated and getting good sleep), some are weekly (e.g., participating in corporate worship, exercising for 150 minutes each week), and others are annual or semiannual (e.g., attending a silent retreat). I have created posters with my rule of life as visible reminders. One is posted in my office, another in my bedroom. Habakkuk teaches us the wisdom of writing a vision and making it plain enough for a runner to see. For those of us whose excessive busyness keeps us on the run, the Self-Care Rule of Life is the vision for the appointed time that we need.

Today's Practice

Begin developing a personal rule of life using the guidelines in the back of this book (see "Self-Care Rule of Life Planning Guide"). Be prayerful in discerning this. Start small. You want this to be challenging but realistic, not idealistic. It is good to start with what you are already doing (think back to day 4 of this study, when you identified your existing practices). Then add any practices that have been helpful over the past seven weeks. If you want to heighten your practice, create a poster of your rule of life and put copies in places where it can serve as a reminder to you. Make a commitment to review it at appointed times of the year. When needed, revise it to reflect your current self-care needs and realities.

Resurrecting Self-Care

"Come to me, all you who are struggling hard and carrying heavy loads, and I will give you rest. Put on my yoke, and learn from me. I'm gentle and humble. And you will find rest for yourselves. My yoke is easy to bear, and my burden is light."

MATTHEW 11:28–30

Week in Review

I am still looking for Jesus's yoke. You know, the one that he promises is light and easy. I have yet to find much that is light or easy about Christian leadership. As a seminary student, a seminary professor, and a congregational leader, I have felt more weighed down by the demands of ministry since following the call twenty years ago than I did during my clinical psychology training and career. Under the banner of "take up thy cross," modern Western Christianity often places excessive and unjust burdens upon us to prove our worth and faithfulness before God.

If Christ's yoke is supposed to lighten, rather than amplify, our load, then maybe we have been wearing the wrong yokes. Perhaps we have been wearing the yoke of capitalism, which teaches us that our worth is in what we produce and consume. Maybe we have been saddled with the yoke of legalism, with its unending rules about what we have to do to merit entry into the kingdom of heaven. Perhaps we have been wearing the yoke of White supremacist heteropatriarchal ableism, which teaches us that our Blackness, our femaleness, our queerness, our disability, our neurodivergence, or our immigration status are shortcomings we have to atone for. Or maybe we have been wearing the yoke of Christian martyrdom and we have forgotten that while self-sacrifice is sometimes the inevitable consequence of living into our Christian identity, it is never the goal.

We have been wearing the wrong yoke. Ours is not the faith that ends in a tomb on Good Friday. It is the faith that greets an empty tomb on Easter Sunday. It is the faith that meets a risen Christ who bids us to rise with him. This is the faith that sacred self-care helps us to live into—resurrecting faith.

My prayer is that this book will be a pathway to our seeing the yokes that we already bear, including the unjust yokes that the world places upon us and that we place upon ourselves. As we see them, we can remove them and make room for the yoke that Jesus has promised us, the one that is easy and light.

Silent Reflection

Spend some time reflecting upon your experience with this book. What have you learned? What improvements have you made in your self-care practices? What changes and supports have made these improvements possible for you? What do you hope to carry with you as you go forward? How will you remind yourself of and hold yourself accountable to your self-care commitments in an ongoing, consistent way?

Prayer

God of resurrection, we confess that as moths drawn to flame, we have been drawn to habits of living that threaten to destroy us. Forgive us, we pray. Liberate us from our constant striving and from unjust burdens. Help us to see ourselves and all of humanity as endowed with sacred worth that does not come from our hustle but from you alone. Free us for joyful obedience to your Sabbath command, and empower us to care for ourselves and all of creation in the way that you care for us. Amen.

Hymn

SPIRIT OF THE LIVING GOD
African American Heritage Hymnal, #320

Spirit of the Living God,
Fall fresh on me,
Spirit of the Living God,
Fall fresh on me.
Break me, melt me, mold me, fill me.
Spirit of the Living God,
Fall fresh on me.

Benediction

May the spirit of the living Christ fall fresh on you, inviting you into a new way of life, one in which you abound in care and love for yourself, for humanity, and for all of creation. Go forth with the assurance that God's love for you is for you. Dwell in that love as you seek to love your neighbor and to love God. Be revived, be renewed, be resurrected! Amen.

Acknowledgments

This book has been twenty years in the making. When I taught my first self-care class to the women's ministry at Compassion Ministries of Durham, I started a new folder on my computer entitled "Untitled Self-Care Manuscript." I thought it would be my first and only book. But then life happened. I heard my call to ministry (in the middle of one of those women's ministry sessions), went to seminary, became a seminary professor, and wrote a few other books. Along the way, people kept asking when I was going to write a book about self-care. I wish I had kept track of all of them, because I would thank them here. This will have to do: to all of you who kept encouraging me when I wasn't sure I had enough wisdom to write on this topic, thank you.

I am deeply grateful to the people who followed the Resurrecting Self-Care Lent challenge, first on Instagram in 2021 and then on Facebook in 2022. Special thanks go to my friends Mayra Macedo-Nolan and Kathryn Broyles, both of whom texted me in the middle of the challenge in 2021 and said, "You know this is a book, right?"

Over the years, I have had the chance to test this material with multiple groups, including the students in my mindfulness and self-care class at Columbia Theological Seminary and the Faith in Action Black Women's Caucus. Thanks also to my research assistant at Columbia, Tsharre Sanders, who helped me think through the hymns and biblical references for this book.

I am extremely proud that this book is the first represented by my agent, Rachelle Gardner of Gardner Literary. Thank you for believing in me and in this project. And I cannot extend enough appreciation to Kathryn "Katy" Hamilton, Chantal Tom, and the entire HarperOne team for shepherding this book so skillfully. All of you have helped this academic pursue the type of writing that I'm most passionate about.

This book and my life would be incomplete without Delwin and Micah. Their imprint is on everything I do. I hope I make them proud.

Above all, I want to thank God, who never lets me write anything without living it first. I pray that I've been faithful in my witness.

Sacred Self-Care Inventory

This worksheet is designed to help you assess and reflect upon your current self-care behaviors. The list is not exhaustive but is a starting point for assessing your self-care practices. There is no scoring and no expectation that you should be doing all of these. When you are done, pay attention without judgment to the patterns in your responses. What areas are you doing well in? Where could you use improvement?

Use the scale below to rate each item.

3	I do this consistently or on a regular basis.
2	I do this sometimes.
1	I rarely do this.
0	I never do this.

Spiritual Self-Care	3 Consistently	2 Sometimes	1 Rarely	0 Never
Devote time to prayer and scripture reading				
Practice meditation or centering prayer				
Participate in corporate worship or scripture study				
Set aside a day for reflection and renewal				
Take time to experience the beauty of God in nature				
Participate in a spiritual community or peer group that challenges and supports me				
Seek spiritual direction				
Express gratitude for my blessings				
Intentionally cultivate a forgiving disposition				
Participate in a multiday retreat				

Physical Self-Care	3 Consistently	2 Sometimes	1 Rarely	0 Never
Drink at least 64oz of water daily				
Take time for meals each day				
Eat in ways that are healthy for my body				
Get at least 7 hours of sleep each night				
Get 150 minutes of moderate to vigorous exercise each week				
Maintain a good balance of activity and rest				
Notice and respond to my body's signals (e.g., pain, fatigue, discomfort)				
Have a good medical support team				
Follow up with medical care				
Properly manage any physical health conditions, illnesses, or disabilities				
Try to accept and love my body				

Emotional Self-Care	3 Consistently	2 Sometimes	1 Rarely	0 Never
Laugh and have fun often				
Find time to do things I enjoy				
Engage in play and creativity				
Participate in therapy				
Journal				
Practice positive self-talk				
Say no and assert boundaries				
Work at a reasonable pace				
Refrain from overcommitting				
Limit social media consumption				
Acknowledge and accept positive and negative emotions				
Appropriately manage mental health conditions, illnesses, or disabilities				
Recognize when I am stressed and respond to it				

Mental Self-Care	3 Consistently	2 Sometimes	1 Rarely	0 Never
Practice mindfulness meditation				
Read books, magazines, or newspapers				
Do puzzles				
Learn or practice a new skill				
Take a class				
Watch documentaries or films that expose me to different cultures				
Learn a language				
Play word games or strategy games				
Attend plays, museums, or cultural performances				
Intentionally expose myself to different viewpoints				
Take time for mental rest				

Relational Self-Care	3 Consistently	2 Sometimes	1 Rarely	0 Never
Spend quality time with people whom I care about and who care about me				
Have friendships based on mutual respect and reciprocity				
Express my gratitude to others				
Call, text, and contact friends and family				
Give and receive compliments				
Be capable of asking for and receiving help from others				
Minimize contact with energy vampires				
Have harmonious relationships with people I live and work with				
Do fun things with other people				

Self-Care Rule
of Life Planning Guide

The Self-Care Rule of Life is a set of activities, habits, disciplines, and practices that foster your spiritual, physical, emotional, mental, and relational wholeness. For Christians, it helps to sustain our vitality as disciples and leaders. As discussed on day 48, it is a worthwhile exercise to spend some time developing your own Self-Care Rule of Life that can help direct your practices and help you maintain them throughout the year. Preparing your Self-Care Rule of Life is a three-step process.

STEP 1:
Identify what you need and
how often you need it.

Think about your needs in each of the following categories. Start with your strengths. Identify what you're already doing and then build upon it. Don't make it too complicated. Your plan should be challenging but also realistic and achievable.

- **Spiritual self-care** consists of the practices you use to nurture your connection to and relationship with the Divine. Be sure to consider both personal experiential disciplines (e.g., prayer, meditation, journaling) and corporate disciplines (e.g., worship,

Bible study, participation in a community of faith). They may be regular or more sporadic events (e.g., attending retreats).

- **Physical self-care** consists of the practices you use to enhance and support your physical well-being. This includes nutrition and hydration, exercise, sleep and rest, sexuality, and body acceptance. If you have any chronic physical health problems or disabilities, be sure to include the medical care and personal behaviors necessary for managing those conditions.

- **Emotional self-care** consists of the practices you use to reflect upon your emotional experiences, manage your reactivity to stress, and increase your sense of pleasure, joy, and self-esteem. This might include enforcing boundaries, being aware of your limits, journaling, mindfulness practices, therapy, support groups, and engaging in play, creativity, and laughter. If you have any mental health challenges, be sure to include the care and supports that you need.

- **Mental self-care** consists of the practices you use to develop, maintain, and enhance mental capacities such as knowledge, attention, critical thinking, memory, communication, creativity, curiosity, and openness. Examples include mindfulness meditation, reading, doing puzzles, learning a new skill, or taking a class. If you are neurodivergent, this will include the strategies and supports that you need to function well in the world.

- **Relational self-care** involves how we develop and nurture relationships that are based upon mutual affection, respect, and reciprocity. Practices include making phone calls, writing letters, sharing meals, spending quality time with loved ones, and showing up for special events.

Notice that there is some overlap between the categories because many practices nurture multiple aspects of ourselves. Mindfulness meditation, for example, is a form of emotional, mental, and spiritual self-care. Don't worry about assigning things to the right category. Do what feels right and good for you.

STEP 2:
Make it visible.

Create a one-page poster that utilizes text and visuals to depict the practices you have identified. For convenience, I have created a Self-Care Rule of Life template that you can edit and print. You can find it in the self-care resource guide at www.drchanequa.com. Once you have printed your rule of life, post it in at least one visible place. I have posted mine above the vanity in my bedroom and also on the wall in my office.

STEP 3:
Revise it.

At least once a year, review and revise your Self-Care Rule of Life. The start of the new year, Lent, and the start of a new academic year are great opportunities to evaluate your existing practices. There may be some that you no longer need and others that you need to add. The revision does not need to be major. Sometimes nothing will change, and that is just fine.

Using This Book
for Lent

As I mentioned in the introduction, much of the content of this book was originally developed to be used during Lent, and if you decide to do so, here is a guide. But first, allow me to share some background.

I did not grow up observing Lent as a liturgical season. Before I went to seminary in 2004, I had never heard of the liturgical calendar. If anyone had asked me, I would have said that the church calendar had four special days: Christmas, Easter, Church Anniversary, and Pastor's Anniversary (maybe Watch Night could have been a fifth). Anything outside of those events would have been my idea of *ordinary time*.

It is not surprising, then, that during February of my first year in seminary, I was confused when I walked onto campus one day and saw a classmate with a black smudge on her forehead. I started to say, "You have something on your forehead," but then I noticed someone else with the same smudge, several people, in fact. They were all White, but beyond that, there was no obvious similarity that might explain why they were choosing to walk around with dirt on their faces. When I entered the classroom, I made my way over to a group of Black classmates, all of whom were Baptist and Pentecostal first-year seminarians. They were just as confused as I was. We whispered among ourselves, not wanting to look stupid by asking one of our White classmates what was happening. Finally, we saw a Black Methodist classmate with the mark. He explained to us that it was the imposition of ashes from the Ash Wednesday service.

I had heard of Ash Wednesday but did not know what it was. Nor did I know its connection to Lent. And until then, I did not know that Lent is a traditional period of fasting and heightened spiritual practice for Christians. Over the next six weeks, I listened as classmates from various mainline Protestant backgrounds talked about their Lenten practices. Some had given up meat, others chocolate, still others sweets of all kinds. "What's the point?" I asked. Some said it was about sacrifice; others said discipline. Eventually, I figured out that Lenten fasts were an invitation to commemorate Christ's forty-day period of fasting in the wilderness—and ultimately his sacrifice of his own life on the cross—by giving up something that we loved. Even giving up something as mundane as chocolate (not actually mundane if you are a middle-aged woman) required a discipline that many people in affluent postindustrial countries lack.

The idea of discipline appealed to me. My father converted to Islam in 1975, just after he and my mother separated. As a Baptist teenager trying to understand my father's faith, I used my first research paper assignment to learn more about the Five Pillars of Islam, the ritual acts considered to be the foundation of Muslim life and identity: the profession of faith, daily prayer, almsgiving, fasting, and the Hajj (the pilgrimage to Mecca). Over the decades, I have had a chance to view Muslim discipline up close. I have sat silently in the car in a mall parking lot with my father and my stepmother's nephew as they halted our shopping excursion in order to pray. I have clumsily tried to follow the prayer postures in the back of the women's room at a Friday afternoon Jum'uah service. I have listened to my stepmother's preteen niece talk about why she wanted to fast that year even though she was not yet at the age of requirement. I have prayed for my father's strength and sustenance as he worked as a brick-layer while observing Ramadan in July heat.

For years, I regretted that Christianity had no parallel to Ramadan. I saw the impact that it had upon my Muslim relatives. It seemed to invigorate their faith and empower them to live out the rest of the year in accordance with their beliefs. I hungered for that sense of piety, even though I was also relieved that I was exempt from the strict practices that my father faithfully observed. When I was introduced to Lent, I realized that the Christian tradition has its own liturgies of abstinence, prayer, and devotion. And as you know from the introduction, starting with my second year in seminary I threw myself headlong into the Lenten observance, something that continues to this day.

...

If you are using this book during Lent, you can use the scripture readings from the Revised Common Lectionary (RCL) to enrich your experience on Sundays and during Holy Week. The lectionary is a three-year cycle of biblical passages used in Sunday worship by many Protestant denominations and churches across the globe, including the African Methodist Episcopal Church, the American Baptist Churches USA, the Christian Church (Disciples of Christ), the Cooperative Baptist Fellowship, the Evan-

gelical Lutheran Church in America, the Mennonite Church, the
Presbyterian Church (U.S.A.), the Episcopal Church, the United
Methodist Church, and the United Church of Christ.

The RCL follows the liturgical calendar, with each year beginning in Advent. Each week includes four readings, usually with
representation from the Hebrew canon (or Old Testament), the
Psalter, the New Testament epistles, and one of the Gospels.
Year A begins on the first Sunday of Advent in 2025, 2028, 2031,
and continuing every third year; Year B begins on the same day
in 2026, 2029, 2032, and so on; and Year C in 2027, 2030,
2033, and so forth. If you feel like doing some math, remember
that Year A always begins in years evenly divisible by three
(e.g., 2025 is evenly divided by three with no remainder).

If you don't attend a church that reads from the RCL each
week, then you probably don't know (or won't remember)
what lectionary year we're in. Don't worry. You can just google
"what lectionary year are we in" or visit Vanderbilt University's
RCL site (https://lectionary.library.vanderbilt.edu). A printable
version of each lectionary year is available at www.common
texts.org/rcl/. For convenience, the lectionary readings for Ash
Wednesday, each Sunday in Lent, Holy Week, and Easter Sunday
are listed in the following table.

DAY/WEEK	YEAR A	YEAR B	YEAR C
Ash Wednesday[*]	Joel 2:1–2, 12–17 or Isaiah 58:1–12 Psalm 51:1–17 2 Corinthians 5:20b–6:10 Matthew 6:1–6, 16–21	Joel 2:1–2, 12–17 or Isaiah 58:1–12 Psalm 51:1–17 2 Corinthians 5:20b–6:10 Matthew 6:1–6, 16–21	Joel 2:1–2, 12–17 or Isaiah 58:1–12 Psalm 51:1–17 2 Corinthians 5:20b–6:10 Matthew 6:1–6, 16–21

1st Sunday in Lent	Genesis 2:15–17; 3:1–7 Psalm 32 Romans 5:12–19 Matthew 4:1–11	Genesis 9:8–17 Psalm 25:1–10 1 Peter 3:18–22 Mark 1:9–15	Deuteronomy 26:1–11 Psalm 91:1–2, 9–16 Romans 10:8b–13 Luke 4:1–13
2nd Sunday in Lent	Genesis 12:1–4a Psalm 121 Romans 4:1–5, 13–17 John 3:1–17 or Matthew 17:1–9	Genesis 17:1–7, 15–16 Psalm 22:23–31 Romans 4:13–25 Mark 8:31–38 or Mark 9:2–9	Genesis 15:1–12, 17–18 Psalm 27 Philippians 3:17–4:1 Luke 13:31–35 or Luke 9:28–36
3rd Sunday in Lent	Exodus 17:1–7 Psalm 95 Romans 5:1–11 John 4:5–42	Exodus 20:1–17 Psalm 19 1 Corinthians 1:18–25 John 2:13–22	Isaiah 55:1–9 Psalm 63:1–8 1 Corinthians 10:1–13 Luke 13:1–9
4th Sunday in Lent	1 Samuel 16:1–13 Psalm 23 Ephesians 5:8–14 John 9:1–41	Numbers 21:4–9 Psalm 107:1–3, 17–22 Ephesians 2:1–10 John 3:14–21	Joshua 5:9–12 Psalm 32 2 Corinthians 5:16–21 Luke 15:1–3, 11b-32
5th Sunday in Lent	Ezekiel 37:1–14 Psalm 130 Romans 8:6–11 John 11:1–45	Jeremiah 31:31–34 Psalm 51:1–12 or Psalm 119:9–16 Hebrews 5:5–10 John 12:20–33	Isaiah 43:16–21 Psalm 126 Philippians 3:4b-14 John 12:1–8
6th Sunday in Lent (Palm Sunday)	Psalm 118:1–2, 19–29 Matthew 21:1–11	Psalm 118:1–2, 19–29 Mark 11:1–11 or John 12:12–16	Psalm 118:1–2, 19–29 Luke 19:28–40
Monday of Holy Week*	Isaiah 42:1–9 Psalm 36:5–11 Hebrews 9:11–15 John 12:1–11	Isaiah 42:1–9 Psalm 36:5–11 Hebrews 9:11–15 John 12:1–11	Isaiah 42:1–9 Psalm 36:5–11 Hebrews 9:11–15 John 12:1–11
Tuesday of Holy Week*	Isaiah 49:1–7 Psalm 71:1–14 1 Corinthians 1:18–31 John 12:20–36	Isaiah 49:1–7 Psalm 71:1–14 1 Corinthians 1:18–31 John 12:20–36	Isaiah 49:1–7 Psalm 71:1–14 1 Corinthians 1:18–31 John 12:20–36

Wednesday of Holy Week*	Isaiah 50:4–9a Psalm 70 Hebrews 12:1–3 John 13:21–32	Isaiah 50:4–9a Psalm 70 Hebrews 12:1–3 John 13:21–32	Isaiah 50:4–9a Psalm 70 Hebrews 12:1–3 John 13:21–32
Thursday of Holy Week (Maundy Thursday)*	Exodus 12:1–4, [5–10], 11–14 Psalm 116:1–2, 12–19 1 Corinthians 11:23–26 John 13:1–17, 31b–35	Exodus 12:1–4, [5–10], 11–14 Psalm 116:1–2, 12–19 1 Corinthians 11:23–26 John 13:1–17, 31b–35	Exodus 12:1–4, [5–10], 11–14 Psalm 116:1–2, 12–19 1 Corinthians 11:23–26 John 13:1–17, 31b–35
Friday of Holy Week (Good Friday)*	Isaiah 52:13–53:12 Psalm 22 Hebrews 10:16–25 or Hebrews 4:14–16; 5:7–9 John 18:1–19:42	Isaiah 52:13–53:12 Psalm 22 Hebrews 10:16–25 or Hebrews 4:14–16; 5:7–9 John 18:1–19:42	Isaiah 52:13–53:12 Psalm 22 Hebrews 10:16–25 or Hebrews 4:14–16; 5:7–9 John 18:1–19:42
Saturday of Holy Week (Holy Saturday)*	Job 14:1–14 or Lamentations 3:1–9, 19–24 Psalm 31:1–4, 15–16 1 Peter 4:1–8 Matthew 27:57–66 or John 19:38–42	Job 14:1–14 or Lamentations 3:1–9, 19–24 Psalm 31:1–4, 15–16 1 Peter 4:1–8 Matthew 27:57–66 or John 19:38–42	Job 14:1–14 or Lamentations 3:1–9, 19–24 Psalm 31:1–4, 15–16 1 Peter 4:1–8 Matthew 27:57–66 or John 19:38–42
Easter Sunday	Acts 10:34–43 or Jeremiah 31:1–6 Psalm 118:1–2, 14–24 Colossians 3:1–4 or Acts 10:34–43 John 20:1–18 or Matthew 28:1–10	Acts 10:34–43 or Isaiah 25:6–9 Psalm 118:1–2, 14–24 1 Corinthians 15:1–11 or Acts 10:34–43 John 20:1–18 or Mark 16:1–8	Acts 10:34–43 or Isaiah 65:17–25 Psalm 118:1–2, 14–24 1 Corinthians 15:19–26 or Acts 10:34–43 John 20:1–18 or Luke 24:1–12

*The readings for Ash Wednesday and Holy Week (except for Easter Sunday) are the same in Years A, B, and C.

NOTES

Introduction: Self-Care as a Way of Life

1. Marjorie J. Thompson, *Soul Feast: An Invitation to the Christian Spiritual Life*, rev. ed. (Louisville, KY: Westminster John Knox Press, 2014), 7.
2. *The African American Heritage Hymnal: 575 Hymns, Spirituals, and Gospel Songs* (Chicago: GIA, 2001) is the first ecumenical hymnal designed to capture the rich musical tradition of the African American Christian experience. One of its distinctions is that its musical notation follows the ways that African American congregations traditionally sing the hymns, which often differs from the notation in other hymnals.
3. The lectionary is a three-year cycle of biblical passages used in Sunday worship by many Protestant denominations and churches across the globe. It follows the liturgical calendar, with each year beginning in Advent.

DAY 5: Self-Care Is Subversive

1. Audre Lorde, *A Burst of Light and Other Essays* (Mineola, NY: Ixia Press, 1988), 130.

DAY 6: Self-Care Is Reparative

1. Bessel A. van der Kolk provides an extensive review of this literature in his bestselling book, *The Body Keeps the Score: Brain, Mind, and Body in the Healing of Trauma* (New York: Penguin Books, 2014). For a summary of the development of research on the intergenerational transmission of trauma among Holocaust survivors, see Rachel Yehuda, "Trauma in the Family Tree," *Scientific American* 327, no. 1 (July 2022): 50–55. Another great resource is the CDC-Kaiser Permanente Adverse Childhood Experiences (ACE) Study, which has significantly advanced our understanding of the impact of trauma by demonstrating that adverse and traumatic situations experienced during childhood have significant

impact upon our health as adults. For the original study, see Vincent J. Felitti et al., "Relationship of Childhood Abuse and Household Dysfunction to Many of the Leading Causes of Death in Adults: The Adverse Childhood Experiences (ACE) Study," *American Journal of Preventive Medicine* 14, no. 4 (May 1998): 245–258, https://doi.org/10.1016/S0749-3797(98)00017-8.

DAY 8: Water to Live

1. Lorenzo Cohen and Alison Jefferies, *Anticancer Living: Transform Your Life and Health with the Mix of Six* (New York: Viking, 2018), 259.

DAY 10: Rest for Your Soul

1. Cohen and Jefferies, *Anticancer Living*, 176–177.

DAY 17: Befriend Your Inner Critic

1. Kristin Neff, *Self-Compassion: The Proven Power of Being Kind to Yourself* (New York: William Morrow, 2011), 34.

DAY 18: Affirm Your Enoughness

1. I describe the myth of the StrongBlackWoman and its impact upon the health and well-being of Black women in *Too Heavy a Yoke: Black Women and the Burden of Strength* (Eugene, OR: Cascade Books, 2014).

DAY 22: No Boundaries, No Self-Care

1. Erikson described the eight stages of psychosocial development in his text *Childhood and Society* (New York: W. W. Norton, 1950; repr., 1968, 1985). He further expounded upon the issue of adolescent identity development in *Identity: Youth and Crisis* (New York: W. W. Norton, 1968). His theory is considered to be the most influential theory of lifespan psychosocial development. See Curtis S. Dunkel and Colin Harbke, "A Review of Measures of Erikson's Stages of Psychosocial Development: Evidence for a General Factor," *Journal of Adult Development* 24, no. 1 (March 2017): 58–76, https://doi.org/10.1007/s10804-016-9247-4.

DAY 26: Protect Your Energy

1. Judith Orloff, *Positive Energy: 10 Extraordinary Prescriptions for Transforming Fatigue, Stress, and Fear into Vibrance, Strength, and Love* (New York: Three Rivers Press, 2004).

DAY 33: Laughter Is Medicine

1. Catherine M. MacDonald, "A Chuckle a Day Keeps the Doctor Away: Therapeutic Humor and Laughter," *Journal of Psychosocial Nursing and Mental Health Services* 42, no. 3 (March 2004): 18–25, https://doi.org/10.3928/02793695-20040315-05.
2. Nilgün Kuru Alici and Ayse Arikan Dönmez, "A Systematic Review of the Effect of Laughter Yoga on Physical Function and Psychosocial Outcomes in Older Adults," *Complementary Therapies in Clinical Practice* 41 (November 2020): 101252, https://doi.org/10.1016/j.ctcp.2020.101252; Maria Meier et al., "Laughter Yoga Reduces the Cortisol Response to Acute Stress in Healthy Individuals," *Stress* 24, no. 1 (2021): 44–52, https://doi.org/10.1080/10253890.2020.1766018; Raquel Oliveira and Patrícia Arriaga, "A Systematic Review of the Effects of Laughter on Blood Pressure and Heart Rate Variability," *Humor: International Journal of Humor Research* 35, no. 2 (2022): 135–167, https://doi.org/10.1515/humor-2021-0111.

DAY 34: The Power of Play and Creativity

1. Aqila Liyana Abdul Rauf and Kamariah Abu Bakar, "Effects of Play on the Social Development of Preschool Children," *Creative Education* 10, no. 12 (November 2019): 2640–2648; Melinda Wenner, "The Serious Need for Play," *Scientific American Mind* 20, no. 1 (February/March 2009): 22–29.

DAY 37: Mindfulness Matters

1. Jon Kabat-Zinn, "Mindfulness-Based Interventions in Context: Past, Present, and Future," *Clinical Psychology: Science and Practice* 10, no. 2 (2003): 145, https://doi.org/10.1093/clipsy.bpg016.

DAY 40: Wise Speech

1. Pamela Ayo Yetunde and Cheryl A. Giles, eds., introduction to *Black and Buddhist: What Buddhism Can Teach Us About Race, Resilience, Transformation, and Freedom* (Boulder, CO: Shambhala, 2020), 5.

DAY 42: The Skilled Mind

1. The Atlanta child murders were the killings of twenty-nine Black children between 1979 and 1981. Although the alleged killer, Wayne Williams, was arrested and convicted of two murders in 1982, the rest remain unsolved, and there is considerable debate about whether Williams was responsible for all of them. Audra D. S. Burch, "Who Killed Atlanta's Children?," *New York Times*, April 30, 2019, https://www.nytimes.com/2019/04/30/us/atlanta-child-murders.html; James Baldwin, *The Evidence of Things Not Seen* (New York: Henry Holt, 1995).
2. Tayari Jones's novel *Leaving Atlanta* vividly depicts the impact of the murders upon Atlanta's Black children and families (New York: Warner Books, 2002).

RECOMMENDED RESOURCES

For Further Reading

Barton, Ruth Haley. *Sacred Rhythms: Arranging Our Lives for Spiritual Transformation*. Downers Grove, IL: InterVarsity Press, 2009.

Brueggemann, Walter. *Sabbath as Resistance: Saying No to the Culture of Now*. Louisville, KY: Westminster John Knox Press, 2014.

Burkeman, Oliver. *Four Thousand Weeks: Time Management for Mortals*. New York: Farrar, Straus and Giroux, 2021.

Cohen, Lorenzo, and Alison Jefferies. *Anticancer Living: Transform Your Life and Health with the Mix of Six*. New York: Viking, 2018.

Curtice, Kaitlin B. *Living Resistance: An Indigenous Vision for Seeking Wholeness Every Day*. Grand Rapids, MI: Brazos Press, 2023.

Hersey, Tricia. *Rest Is Resistance: A Manifesto*. New York: Little, Brown Spark, 2022.

Jones, Kirk Byron. *Rest in the Storm: Self-Care Strategies for Clergy and Other Caregivers*. Valley Forge, PA: Judson Press, 2021.

Kinsey, Dalia. *Decolonizing Wellness: A QTBIPOC-Centered Guide to Escape the Diet Trap, Heal Your Self-Image, and Achieve Body Liberation*. Dallas, TX: BenBella Books, 2022.

Neff, Kristin. *Self-Compassion: The Proven Power of Being Kind to Yourself*. New York: William Morrow, 2011.

Oden, Amy G. *Right Here, Right Now: The Practice of Christian Mindfulness*. Nashville, TN: Abingdon Press, 2017.

Ortiz, Naomi. *Sustaining Spirit: Self-Care for Social Justice*. Berkeley, CA: Reclamation Press, 2018.

Owens, Lama Rod. *Love and Rage: The Path of Liberation Through Anger*. Berkeley, CA: North Atlantic Books, 2020.

Paintner, Christine Valters. *The Wisdom of the Body: A Contemplative Journey to Wholeness for Women*. Notre Dame, IN: Sorin Books, 2017.

Paulsell, Stephanie. *Honoring the Body: Meditations on a Christian Practice.* Minneapolis, MN: Fortress Press, 2019.

Proeschold-Bell, Rae Jean, and Jason Byassee. *Faithful and Fractured: Responding to the Clergy Health Crisis.* Grand Rapids, MI: Baker Academic, 2018.

Raheem, Octavia F. *Pause, Rest, Be: Stillness Practices for Courage in Times of Change.* Boulder, CO: Shambhala, 2022.

Scazzero, Peter. *Emotionally Healthy Spirituality: It's Impossible to Be Spiritually Mature While Remaining Emotionally Immature.* Grand Rapids, MI: Zondervan, 2006.

Stucky, Nathan T. *Wrestling with Rest: Inviting Youth to Discover the Gift of Sabbath.* Grand Rapids, MI: Wm. B. Eerdmans, 2019.

Swenson, Richard A. *Margin: Restoring Emotional, Physical, Financial, and Time Reserves to Overloaded Lives.* Colorado Springs, CO: NavPress, 2004.

Tawwab, Nedra Glover. *Set Boundaries, Find Peace: A Guide to Reclaiming Yourself.* New York: TarcherPerigee, 2021.

Taylor, Barbara Brown. *An Altar in the World: A Geography of Faith.* New York: HarperCollins, 2009.

Taylor, Sonya Renee. *The Body Is Not an Apology: The Power of Radical Self-Love.* Oakland, CA: Berrett-Koehler, 2018.

Van der Kolk, Bessel A. *The Body Keeps the Score: Brain, Mind, and Body in the Healing of Trauma.* New York: Penguin Books, 2014.

Walker-Barnes, Chanequa. *Too Heavy a Yoke: Black Women and the Burden of Strength.* Eugene, OR: Cascade Books, 2014.

Winner, Lauren F. *Mudhouse Sabbath: An Invitation to a Life of Spiritual Discipline.* Brewster, MA: Paraclete Press, 2003.

Mindfulness Meditation Classes and Apps

UMass Center for Mindfulness

- Home of the original Mindfulness-Based Stress Reduction (MBSR) program developed by Jon Kabat-Zinn. Offers online and in-person classes. Classes are nonsectarian and appropriate for all religious and spiritual backgrounds.

- https://www.ummhealth.org/umass-memorial-medical-center/
  services-treatments/center-for-mindfulness

Mindfulness Center at Brown
- Offers online and in-person classes, including weekly meditations, MBSR, and MBSR teacher training. Classes are nonsectarian and appropriate for all religious and spiritual backgrounds.
- https://www.brown.edu/public-health/mindfulness/home

Insight Meditation Society
- Offers online and in-person classes and retreats grounded in the Buddhist Vipassana (Insight) tradition. Classes are open to people of all religious and spiritual backgrounds.
- https://www.dharma.org

Insight Timer Meditation App
- Free meditation app that includes more than 130,000 guided meditations from a wide variety of traditions, including Christian mindfulness, MBSR practices, and more.
- https://insighttimer.com